Anxiety Reset

A 90-DAY GUIDED JOURNAL & WORKBOOK

to Calm Your Mind, Rewire Your Thoughts & Reclaim Inner Peace

SOPHIA GRACE

D1713923

CONTENT

PART I: A GREETING FROM THE HEART

PART II: THE 12-WEEK JOURNEY

PART III: TOOLKIT FROM THE HEART

PART IV: FAREWELL & RESOURCES

DISCLAIMER

This journal is a supportive self-help tool and is not intended to diagnose, treat, or replace professional mental health care. The exercises, prompts, and suggestions provided are inspired by therapeutic principles (such as CBT, mindfulness, and somatic practices), but are offered for reflection and education only.

Everyone's healing journey is unique. If you are experiencing severe anxiety, panic attacks, trauma responses, or any form of emotional crisis, please seek support from a qualified therapist, counselor, or medical provider.

The author and publisher are not responsible for any outcomes resulting from the use or misuse of the content within this journal.

Use this journal gently, with compassion, and in a way that honors your current capacity. Remember that healing is not linear—and you are exactly where you need to be. Let's begin this journey together, one page at a time.

CALM MIND ESSENTIALS KIT

A COMPANION FOR YOUR HEALING JOURNEY

Before you open your first page, I'd love to offer you something extra — a free gift created to support and guide you through your healing journey.

Calm Mind Essentials Kit: Printable affirmations, emotional grounding techniques, a feelings map, and shadow work templates — designed to meet you wherever you are.

Visit: https://short.com.vn/eRBM

(Or scan the QR code below to access your free kit.)

May your journey be filled with patience, courage, and compassion.

PART I

A GREETING FROM THE HEART

WE BEGIN HERE

A COMPASSIONATE WELCOME

Dear Friend,

If this journal is in your hands right now, perhaps your heart is seeking companionship. Maybe your breath sometimes becomes hurried, your mind races too quickly, and your body carries tensions that others cannot see.

I see you. I see the silent battle you're experiencing. Those moments when anxiety rises, when your heart beats faster, when thoughts circle endlessly, and when you feel like you're standing alone in the storm.

But here, within these pages, you are no longer alone.

This journal isn't a miracle or a perfect solution. It's a companion on a 90-day journey where we'll explore, feel, and gradually rediscover the peace within. A safe space where you can set down your burdens and find your breath again.

WHAT THIS JOURNAL IS

This is not a magical fix. This is not a way to "repair" what isn't broken.

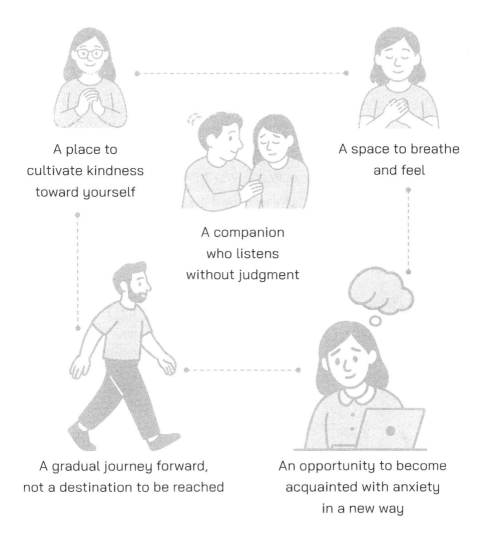

A place to
cultivate kindness
toward yourself

A companion
who listens
without judgment

A space to breathe
and feel

A gradual journey forward,
not a destination to be reached

An opportunity to become
acquainted with anxiety
in a new way

Each page is an invitation to be honest about what's happening within you, to listen to your needs, and to nurture the seeds of peace.

A PROMISE

With an open heart, I want to offer you a promise:

There are no failure days on this journey.

Each day you open this journal, even if just to touch it or read a line, that's a step. Every moment you turn to these pages, whether your mind is peaceful or stormy, that's courage.

You don't need to complete every exercise. You don't need to write every day. You don't need to feel "better" on a fixed schedule.

Instead, I invite you to come here exactly as you are, with everything you're carrying. Let this journal serve YOU, not the other way around.

GENTLE WORDS FROM THOSE WHO HAVE WALKED WITH ANXIETY

"Day by day, I learned to embrace my anxiety instead of running from it. It taught me that every emotion has its own message, and when I listened, I found wisdom I didn't know I had."
- Sarah, 34

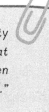

"Anxiety was once my enemy. Now I understand it's a part of me trying to protect me. When I treat it with compassion, it gradually becomes gentler, as if it just needed to be heard." - Michael, 29

"I used to feel ashamed of my worries. But when I started sharing, I realized I wasn't alone. There are people who understand, and that changes everything." - Helena, 42

"Breath has been my best friend on this journey. When I return to it, I find moments of peace even on the hardest days." - Thomas, 38

UNDERSTANDING YOUR JOURNEY

WHAT ANXIETY IS

Anxiety, in its gentlest definition, is a wave in the ocean of human emotion. Sometimes a small ripple, sometimes a fierce surge. It's not a sign of weakness or failure—it's a natural part of our human experience.

ANXIETY OFTEN ARRIVES WHEN:

Our bodies are responding to stress, whether present or from the past

Our minds are trying to protect us from something

Life is changing, and we're stepping into the unknown

Our hearts feel unsafe

We're carrying more than we can process alone

At its core, anxiety is a messenger. Sometimes the message is clear: "Danger ahead!" Other times, it speaks in riddles we need time to understand. But it always deserves our gentle attention.

What anxiety is NOT: **It is not your identity. It is not your fault. It is not a life sentence. And it is not something you need to face alone.**

UNDERSTANDING ANXIETY BETTER

Anxiety isn't just a feeling - it's a complex experience that encompasses thoughts, emotions, and physical reactions. Understanding anxiety better can help us approach it with more compassion and wisdom.

1. THE FACES OF ANXIETY

Anxiety can appear in many different forms. You might recognize some of these:

1. Generalized Anxiety:

Persistent worrying, excessive concern about various issues in daily life, often accompanied by feelings of tension and difficulty concentrating.

2. Panic:

Sudden episodes of high-intensity anxiety with strong physical symptoms like rapid heartbeat, difficulty breathing, and feelings of impending danger.

3. Social Anxiety:

Intense fear of being evaluated, judged, or embarrassed in social situations.

4. Performance Anxiety:

Nervousness when having to perform, speak in public, or work under pressure.

5. Health Anxiety:

Excessive worry about your health, frequent fears about illness despite no medical evidence.

6. Separation Anxiety:

Intense fear when separated from loved ones or familiar spaces.

2. ANXIETY IN THE BODY

When we're anxious, the body often responds in ways that might feel concerning, but are actually completely natural:

Fight or Flight Response: **Our bodies are "wired" to respond to threats by preparing to fight or flee. This is an ancient survival mechanism — very useful when facing a tiger, but not always appropriate for modern stresses like work emails or social media.**

COMMON PHYSIOLOGICAL CHANGES DURING ANXIETY:

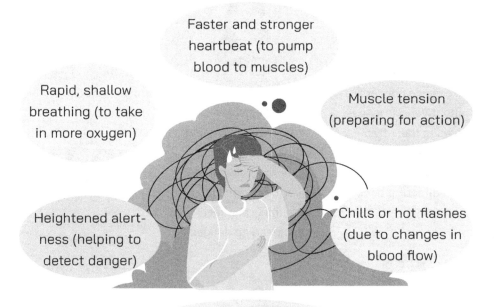

Faster and stronger heartbeat (to pump blood to muscles)

Rapid, shallow breathing (to take in more oxygen)

Muscle tension (preparing for action)

Heightened alertness (helping to detect danger)

Chills or hot flashes (due to changes in blood flow)

Changes in the digestive system (that's why anxiety often affects our stomachs)

When you experience these symptoms, remember that your body isn't broken - it's trying to protect you. Recognizing and naming what's happening can help reduce fear about these sensations themselves.

Anxiety often operates in a self-perpetuating cycle:

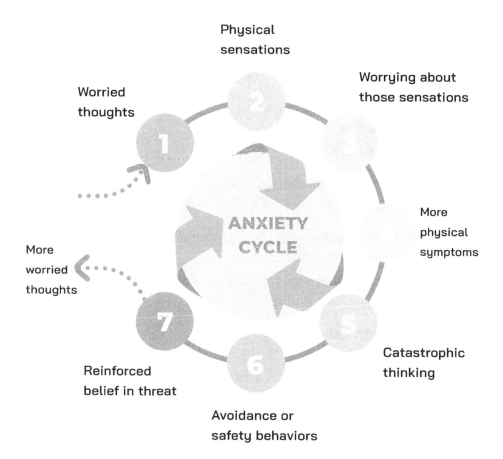

Physical sensations

Worrying about those sensations

Worried thoughts

More physical symptoms

More worried thoughts

ANXIETY CYCLE

Catastrophic thinking

Reinforced belief in threat

Avoidance or safety behaviors

At any point in this cycle, we can intervene. Sometimes just recognizing "Aha, this is the anxiety cycle" can help disrupt it.

Anxiety is often fueled by familiar thought patterns:

• **CATASTROPHIZING:** Imagining the worst-case scenario
("If I mess up this presentation, I'll get fired and never find work again.")

• **MIND READING:** Assuming you know what others are thinking, usually something negative
("Everyone in the room thinks I'm stupid.")

• **BINARY THINKING:** Seeing things in either-or, black-and-white terms
("Either I do this perfectly, or I'm a complete failure.")

• **NEGATIVE FILTERING:** Focusing only on negative details and overlooking positives
("Even though they praised my report, they asked one difficult question - that proves it was really bad.")

FUTURE PREDICTION: Believing you know what will happen, usually something negative
("I know this meeting is going to be terrible.")

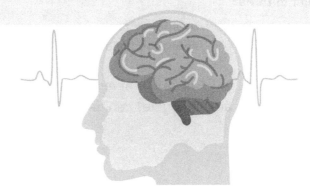

Recognizing these thought patterns doesn't mean you can immediately change them. But awareness is the first step toward viewing thoughts with less identification. They're just thoughts, not facts.

5. WHY DO SOME PEOPLE EXPERIENCE MORE ANXIETY?

Anxiety, like many human experiences, often stems from a complex combination of factors:

- **GENETICS**: Some people have a genetic predisposition to anxiety, just as some people are taller than others. This isn't anyone's fault - it's simply part of human biological diversity.

- **TEMPERAMENT**: From birth, we have different temperaments. Some people are naturally more sensitive or cautious with new situations.

- **LIFE EXPERIENCES**: Past experiences - especially stressful, traumatic, or unsafe ones - can make our nervous systems highly alert.

- **CULTURE**: Social pressure, expectations, and cultural norms also play a role in shaping our anxiety.

- **CURRENT STRESS**: Stressors in present life - from relationships to finances, from work to health - can trigger or intensify anxiety.

- **COMPLEXITY OF MODERN LIFE**: In the modern world with social media, 24/7 news, and constant pressure to work and succeed, we're asking our brains to process more input than ever before.

However, the most important understanding might be: Anxiety isn't your fault, but your response to it can be your choice.

6. THE DIFFERENCE BETWEEN "NORMAL" ANXIETY AND ANXIETY THAT NEEDS HELP

Everyone experiences anxiety - it's a natural and even useful part of life. But sometimes, anxiety can become too overwhelming:

ANXIETY MIGHT NEED PROFESSIONAL SUPPORT WHEN:

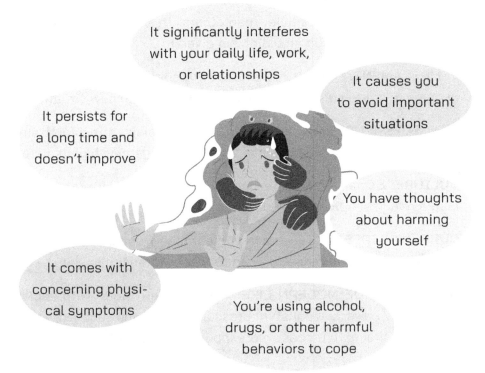

It significantly interferes with your daily life, work, or relationships

It causes you to avoid important situations

It persists for a long time and doesn't improve

You have thoughts about harming yourself

It comes with concerning physical symptoms

You're using alcohol, drugs, or other harmful behaviors to cope

If you're experiencing any of the above, we encourage you to seek support from a mental health professional. This journal can be an excellent supplementary tool, but it doesn't replace professional care.

7. IS ANXIETY THE ENEMY?

In modern society, we're often taught that anxiety is something to be "fought," "overcome," or "cured." But there's another perspective, one that many ancient cultures and many modern approaches share:

Anxiety, at its core, is a protection system. It's a part of the human body that has helped us survive as a species. It awakens the senses, focuses attention, and motivates us to care for what we cherish.

Instead of seeing anxiety as the enemy, we might try viewing it as an overzealous guard - a protector who sometimes gives false alarms, but only because they very much want to keep us safe.

The approach to anxiety this journal suggests isn't about "eliminating" it, but developing a different relationship with it - a relationship characterized by understanding, patience, and even gratitude for the protective intention behind uncomfortable feelings.

8. GOOD NEWS ABOUT ANXIETY

While the journey with anxiety can be challenging, there is some good news worth sharing:

- **ANXIETY CAN CHANGE:** Research shows the brain has "neuroplasticity" - the ability to change and adapt throughout our lives. This means that patterns of anxiety, no matter how long they've existed, can be modified.

- **YOU ARE NOT YOUR ANXIETY:** Anxiety is part of your experience, but it doesn't define who you are. Creating space between yourself and anxiety is an important step toward freedom.

- **KINDNESS HELPS.** Research shows that self-compassion - treating yourself with the kindness you would offer a good friend - can significantly reduce anxiety over time.

- **SIMPLE SKILLS CAN MAKE A BIG DIFFERENCE:** Techniques like conscious breathing, mindfulness, and grounding practices not only help in difficult moments but build resilience over time.

- **YOU ARE NOT ALONE:** Anxiety is one of the most common mental health issues, affecting millions of people. Whenever you feel alone in your struggle, remember that countless others are practicing similar skills and seeking peace just like you.

With all this knowledge, let's continue the journey - not to "fix" anxiety, but to develop a new relationship with it, one based on understanding, kindness and ultimately the wisdom it can bring when we listen with an open heart.

THE 90-DAY JOURNEY

This journey isn't a straight line from anxiety to peace. It's more like a winding river that sometimes flows smoothly, sometimes creates whirlpools, sometimes slows to a gentle meandering.

Over these 90 days, we'll navigate this river together. Each week carries a theme, an invitation to explore different aspects of anxiety and different pathways to peace:

We'll begin by meeting your anxiety face-to-face, then explore the refuge of breath, the wisdom of your body, and practices for staying grounded. We'll listen to the voices within, expand your capacity for feeling, take small brave steps, and cultivate self-compassion. We'll connect with joy, discover your inner strength, build a loving life, and chart the path forward.

Each day is a single step. Each week opens a new door. And the entire journey unfolds at your pace, honoring your unique experience.

YOU ARE NOT ALONE

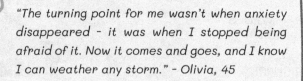

"Anxiety makes us feel isolated in a crowded room. But the truth is, we're all experiencing versions of the same human struggles. When I realized this, I could finally exhale." - James, 31

"The turning point for me wasn't when anxiety disappeared - it was when I stopped being afraid of it. Now it comes and goes, and I know I can weather any storm." - Olivia, 45

"The kindest thing I ever did was to stop fighting myself. When I began treating my anxiety with tenderness instead of frustration, everything shifted." - Rebecca, 39

Millions of people walk with anxiety every day. You're standing in a circle of shared experience that spans across time, cultures, and backgrounds. In this moment, countless others are taking deep breaths, practicing grounding techniques, writing in journals like this one, and seeking their way back to calm.

You are part of a community of hearts learning to hold their humanity with greater compassion.

THE WHISPERS OF ANXIETY

Sometimes anxiety speaks in a language that's hard to understand. Below are some common "whispers" anxiety might bring, and what they might be trying to tell us beneath the surface:

- When anxiety whispers: *"Something terrible is about to happen."*
  It might be saying: "I want you to be safe. I'm trying to protect you."

- When anxiety whispers: *"You're not prepared enough."*
  It might be saying: "This matters to you. You care about doing well."

- When anxiety whispers: *"Everyone is judging you."*
  It might be saying: "Connection is important to you. You value belonging."

- When anxiety whispers: *"You can't handle this."*
  It might be saying: "You've been carrying a lot. You might need rest or support."

- When anxiety whispers: *"What if you fail?"*
  It might be saying: "You're facing something meaningful that requires courage."

What whispers do you hear from your anxiety? And if you listen closely, with compassion rather than fear, what might they be trying to tell you?

....

....

....

....

....

....

....

....

....

....

....

....

....

....

....

....

....

YOUR SAFE SPACE

PERMISSION SLIPS

On this journey, I invite you to give yourself permission—to feel, to rest, to be imperfect, to need help, to change your mind, to take your time.

COMPLETE THESE PERMISSION SLIPS AS A GIFT TO YOURSELF:

I give myself permission to
....
....
....

I give myself permission to
....
....
....

I give myself permission to
....
....
....

I give myself permission to
....
....
....

WHAT I NEED
YOU TO UNDERSTAND

Everyone's experience with anxiety is unique. What triggers anxiety, how it feels in your body, what helps and what doesn't—all of these are personal to each individual.

This is a space for you to express what you want others to understand about your anxiety experience. This might be something you've never said aloud, something you wish your loved ones understood, or something you're just beginning to realize about yourself.

Please complete the sentence below:

What I want others to understand about my anxiety:

....

....

....

....

....

....

....

....

....

....

ME AND MY JOURNEY

To begin this journey together, let's take a moment to connect with where you are right now. There are no right or wrong answers—only your truth in this moment.

Right now, my relationship with anxiety feels like:

....

....

....

....

....

....

The most challenging part of anxiety for me is:

....

....

....

....

....

....

....

A small thing that brings me comfort when I'm anxious:

....
....
....
....
....
....

One way I've been strong in the face of anxiety:

....
....
....
....
....
....

Something I hope to discover or develop through this journal:

....
....
....
....
....
....

A PROMISE TO MYSELF

As you begin this 90-day journey, consider making a simple promise to yourself—not a rigid goal or demand, but a gentle commitment to your own wellbeing.

Dear Self,

During our time with this journal, I promise to:

....

....

....

I make this promise knowing that some days will be easier than others. On the difficult days, I will remember that:

....

....

....

This journey is a gift I'm giving myself because:

....

....

....

With compassion.

PART II

THE
12-WEEK
JOURNEY

WEEK 01

MEETING YOUR ANXIETY

HELLO, ANXIETY

Anxiety isn't an enemy to be defeated, but a part of you trying to protect you in its own way. In this exercise, we'll help you personify your anxiety - not to create more separation, but to create space for dialogue and understanding.

Imagine your anxiety as a character. What does it look like? How does it move? What kind of voice does it speak with? If you'd like, you can draw it in the space below, or simply describe it in words.

[Space for drawing/writing]

WRITE A LETTER TO YOUR ANXIETY:

Dear Anxiety,

....

....

....

....

....

....

....

....

....

....

....

....

....

....

....

....

....

....

Now, imagine your anxiety writing back to you. What might it want to say? Let your hand write without thinking too much. Sometimes the deepest wisdom comes from spontaneous moments.

Dear ....,

....

....

....

....

....

....

....

....

....

....

....

....

....

....

ANXIETY IN MY BODY

Anxiety doesn't just exist in the mind - it lives in our bodies. Each person experiences anxiety differently: racing heart, shaky hands, tension in the shoulders, heaviness in the stomach, or countless other sensations.

Recognizing how anxiety manifests in your body is the first step to responding to it more kindly.

Below is a simple outline of a human body. Using colored pens (if available), color in the areas where you feel anxiety. You can use different colors to represent different types of sensations:

· Red for hot or tense feelings
· Blue for cold or numb sensations
· Yellow for vibrating or shaking sensations
· Green for heavy feelings
· Purple for constricted or tight sensations
· You can also create your own color key

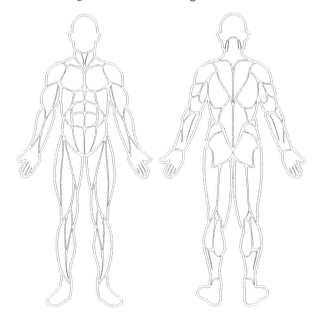

Now, describe what you notice. Where does anxiety first appear in your body? How does it move? Are some areas more tense than others?

....

....

....

....

....

....

....

....

....

....

....

....

....

....

....

....

....

....

LISTENING TO MESSAGES FROM THE BODY:

If these physical sensations could speak, what might they be trying to tell you?

....

....

....

....

....

....

....

A SMALL ACT OF KINDNESS:

Based on what you've discovered, is there a small action you can take right now to care for your body? It might be drinking a glass of water, stretching your shoulders, taking a deep breath, or gently massaging an area of tension.

....

....

....

....

....

....

THE LANGUAGE OF THE HEART VS. THE LANGUAGE OF FEAR

Many of us have two "inner voices" when facing anxiety: the voice of the heart - understanding and compassionate; and the voice of fear - often urgent, critical, and absolute.

Recognizing the difference between these voices can completely change how we experience anxiety.

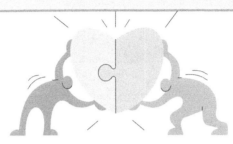

In the anxious situations below, compare how these two voices might respond:

SITUATION 1: YOU FEEL OVERWHELMED WHEN FACING
A LONG TO-DO LIST.

Voice of fear:

....

....

....

Voice of the heart:

....

....

....

SITUATION 2: YOU MAKE A MISTAKE AND WORRY ABOUT HOW OTHERS PERCEIVE YOU.

Voice of fear:

....

....

....

Voice of the heart:

....

....

....

SITUATION 3: YOU FEEL ANXIOUS ABOUT ATTENDING A SOCIAL EVENT.

Voice of fear:

....

....

....

Voice of the heart:

....

....

....

A SITUATION OF YOUR OWN:

....

Voice of fear:

....

....

....

Voice of the heart:

....

....

....

A SITUATION OF YOUR OWN:

....

Voice of fear:

....

....

....

Voice of the heart:

....

....

....

Which voice do you tend to listen to more?

....

....

....

....

....

Which voice creates a lighter feeling in your body?

....

....

....

....

....

How might you cultivate the voice of the heart more in your daily life?

....

....

....

....

....

DAILY REFLECTION 1: THE FIRST MEETING

A TRUE STORY:

When Anna first realized she was living with anxiety, she felt like she was facing an uninvited enemy. Each morning she woke with a heaviness in her chest, wondering: "What's wrong with me?" One day, a friend suggested that instead of fighting against the feeling, Anna might try "inviting it for tea" - treating anxiety like an unexpected guest who might be carrying an important message. The next morning, instead of pushing away the heavy feeling, Anna sat quietly with it and gently asked, "What are you trying to tell me?" She was surprised to realize that the feeling was reminding her about an important project she'd been postponing out of fear of failure. When Anna finally listened, she was not only able to address the practical issue but also began a new relationship with her fear.

Gentle prompt: Today anxiety visited me when...

....

....

....

....

....

....

....

....

Reflection question: If I listen more deeply, what might my anxiety be trying to protect me from?

....

....

....

....

....

....

....

A small moment of peace: Today, I found a glimmer of peace when...

....

....

....

....

....

....

....

....

....

DAILY REFLECTION 2: THE FACES OF ANXIETY

A TRUE STORY:

David always considered himself someone who wasn't anxious - until the day he read about different manifestations of anxiety. He was surprised to realize that his chronic procrastination, excessive perfectionism, and tendency to control in relationships were all masks of anxiety. "I'm not worried," he'd often say, "I'm just being thorough." As David learned to recognize these disguises, he could see that anxiety wasn't just conscious worry - it could hide in everyday behaviors. This awareness opened a new path to self-understanding and developing compassion for parts of himself he used to criticize.

Gentle prompt: Today I noticed my anxiety was "wearing a mask" when I...

....

....

....

....

....

....

....

....

Reflection question: Beneath the surface of this behavior, what might I be seeking?

....

....

....

....

....

....

....

A small step toward kindness: One way I can respond to this actual need with compassion is...

....

....

....

....

....

....

....

....

DAILY REFLECTION 3: LISTENING WITH THE HEART

A TRUE STORY:

Maya always felt like she was racing against time. Whenever anxiety appeared, she immediately jumped into problem-solving mode - researching information, making to-do lists, or seeking advice. One day, in a mindfulness workshop, the facilitator asked her to spend a minute with her hand on her heart, just feeling. At first, Maya felt uncomfortable and impatient. But as she continued the practice, she began to realize that before needing a solution, her heart needed to be heard. Gradually, Maya learned to pause and ask: "What does my heart need in this moment?" Sometimes the answer wasn't an action at all, but simply acknowledgment - "I understand this is hard" or "I am here with you."

Gentle prompt: Today, when anxiety arose, instead of rushing to find a solution, i paused and felt...

....

....

....

....

....

....

....

....

Reflection question: What did my heart truly need in that moment?

....

....

....

....

....

....

....

A gentle word to self: If I could say one thing to my anxious heart, I would say...

....

....

....

....

....

....

....

DAILY REFLECTION 4:
THE WISDOM BEHIND ANXIETY

A TRUE STORY:

Throughout his career, Alex always viewed anxiety as a saboteur of success. The feeling of worry before important meetings, presentations, or even phone calls made him feel weak. Things changed when Alex attended a workshop where the facilitator suggested that anxiety isn't just fear - it can also be a sign of deep caring. "Anxiety and passion often come from the same source," the facilitator shared. "Both show that you're invested in something meaningful." This insight transformed Alex's relationship with anxiety. Instead of seeing it as a sign of inadequacy, he began to view it as an indicator of what truly matters to him. When Alex started asking "What do I care about here?" instead of "Why am I so worried?", he found the wisdom and purpose that anxiety can reveal.

Gentle prompt: Today, my anxiety might be pointing to the fact that I really care about...

....

....

....

....

....

....

....

....

Reflection question: What wisdom or hidden message might be in this anxiety?

....

....

....

....

....

....

....

Transforming perspective: One way I can see this anxiety as a teacher rather than an enemy is...

....

....

....

....

....

....

....

....

ENDING WEEK 1: REFLECTION AND SUMMARY

Three things I've learned about my anxiety this week:

1. ....

....

2. ....

....

3. ....

....

A new way I've viewed or responded to anxiety:

....

....

....

....

....

....

....

The most surprising or interesting thing I discovered:

....

....

....

....

....

....

....

A small intention I'm carrying into next week:

....

....

....

....

....

....

....

REMEMBER: *Meeting your anxiety isn't about making it disappear, but about developing a new relationship - one based on understanding, respect, and ultimately the wisdom it can bring when we listen with an open heart.*

WEEK 02
BREATH AS SANCTUARY

BREATH - THE GIFT ALWAYS PRESENT

In the midst of anxiety's storms, breath is the home we can always return to. It requires no special equipment, private space, or lengthy time commitment. It's here, available to us anytime, anywhere.

Breath is the anchoring cord between mind and body. When anxiety causes our minds to race ahead into a worried future, breath gently pulls us back to the present moment - the only place where we can truly find peace.

This week, we'll explore breath not just as a tool for managing anxiety, but as a companion, a sanctuary, and a wise teacher.

MOMENT OF AWARENESS:

Take a minute to place your hand on your belly and feel your breath. No need to change anything - simply observe. Is your breath deep or shallow? Fast or slow? Smooth or hurried?

Write down what you notice:

....

....

....

REFLECTIONS ON BREATH:

• From birth until we leave this world, breath accompanies us. It is the music of life.

• When we're anxious, breath often becomes shallow and quick. This isn't a sign of failure - it's just information.

• Each moment is an opportunity to begin again with a fresh breath.

BREATH LIKE OCEAN WAVES:

One of the most beautiful ways to visualize breath is to see it like ocean waves - rising and falling, constantly moving in a natural dance.

As we inhale, imagine the wave rising onto the shore. As we exhale, imagine the wave receding, returning to the vast ocean.

PRACTICE OCEAN BREATHING:

1. Find a comfortable position, sitting or lying down.

2. Place one hand on your abdomen, near your navel.

3. As you inhale, allow your belly to rise like a wave coming in.

4. As you exhale, let your belly fall like a wave receding.

5. Continue gently, allowing your body to find its natural rhythm.

6. When thoughts arise (and they will), gently bring attention back to the motion of your breathing waves.

VISUALIZE OCEAN WAVES:

In the space below, you can draw your breath waves, or use words to describe the feeling of practicing ocean breathing.

[Space for drawing/writing]

Bringing ocean breathing into daily life:

What moments in your day could you bring ocean breathing into? Perhaps while sitting in traffic, waiting for an elevator, or before sleep.

....

....

....

PRACTICE CARESSING YOUR BREATH

1. Inhale slowly to a count of 4, imagining that you're gently welcoming new energy.

2. Hold your breath for a count of 4, as if you're embracing the gift of oxygen, allowing it to nourish every cell.

3. Exhale to a count of 4, imagining you're gently releasing everything that no longer serves you.

4. Hold the emptiness for a count of 4, enjoying the perfect moment of stillness.

5. Repeat this cycle 4 times, or as long as feels appropriate.

Draw your box breathing diagram:

In the space below, draw a square. As you practice, let your finger trace around the edges of the square as you inhale, hold, exhale, and hold empty.

[Space to draw a square]

Connect with emotions:

As you practice box breathing, pay attention to subtle changes in your emotional state. Do you notice a gentle relaxation? A small space between you and your anxious thoughts?

....

....

....

....

....

....

....

....

....

....

....

....

....

....

DAILY REFLECTION 1: THE BREATH OF NATURE

A SHORT POEM:

Trees breathe in, breathe out
Never rushing, never blaming
Simply accepting
The rhythm of life.

Rain falls, sun rises
No discrimination, no judgment
Nature simply is
In each passing moment.

Today, I breathe
Like a tree standing in the wind
No need to become someone else
Just present, complete.

Gentle prompt: Today I found a moment of peace when...

....

....

....

....

....

....

....

....

What breath taught me today...

....

....

....

....

....

....

....

A moment with nature: Today, I connected with the natural rhythm of life when...

....

....

....

....

....

....

....

....

....

DAILY REFLECTION 2:
THE BREATH OF GRATITUDE

A SHORT POEM:

Each inhale, a gift
Each exhale, a letting go
No need to search for gratitude afar
It lies within the pulse of life itself.

When complaints arise
Breath gently brings us back
To this simple truth:
We are still breathing, still here.

In every difficult moment
Each breath is a reminder:
Life, though imperfect
Is an immeasurable miracle.

Gentle prompt: Today, I feel grateful for...

....

....

....

....

....

....

....

....

What breath taught me today...

....

....

....

....

....

....

....

A breath of gratitude: As I inhale, I'm grateful for... As I exhale, I release...

....

....

....

....

....

....

....

....

....

DAILY REFLECTION 3:
THE BREATH OF STILLNESS

A SHORT POEM:

Amid the world's noise
There is a silence waiting
No need to search far away
It lies between each inhale and exhale.

When the mind races
Breath is the resting place
A moment to remember that
We are more than hurried thoughts.

In each moment of stillness
We find our true nature
Not what we do
But simply who we are

Gentle prompt: Today I found a moment of stillness when...

....

....

....

....

....

....

....

What breath taught me today...

....

....

....

....

....

....

....

An inner space: When I create space between thought and reaction, I realize...

....

....

....

....

....

....

....

....

DAILY REFLECTION 4:
THE BREATH OF COMPASSION

When pain comes knocking
Often we want to close tight, refuse
But breath opens another way:
No running, no fighting, simply being present.

Breathing In, I acknowledge difficulty
Breathing out, I send gentleness
No need to fix or change
Just holding everything with an open heart.

In each moment of kindness
To self and to others
We find the power of breath:
It doesn't just keep us alive, it teaches us how to live.

Gentle prompt: Today, I offered compassion to myself when...

....

....

....

....

....

....

....

....

What breath taught me today...

....

....

....

....

....

....

....

A compassionate message: If I could say one thing to the suffering part of me, I would say...

....

....

....

....

....

....

....

....

....

BREATHING PRACTICES FOR ANXIOUS MOMENTS:

Below are three simple breathing techniques you can use in moments of anxiety. Practice them when you feel calm so you can easily use them when needed.

1. 4-7-8 Breath

- Inhale through your nose for 4 seconds
- Hold your breath for 7 seconds
- Exhale through your mouth for 8 seconds, making a whooshing sound
- Repeat 3-4 times

Effect: This technique activates the parasympathetic nervous system, helping your body shift from "fight or flight" to "rest and digest."

2. Alternate Nostril Breathing

- Use your right thumb to close your right nostril
- Inhale through your left nostril
- Use your ring finger to close your left nostril
- Exhale through your right nostril
- Inhale through your right nostril
- Close right nostril
- Exhale through left nostril
- This is one cycle; repeat 5-10 times

Effect: Balances the two hemispheres of the brain, helping to create a sense of balance and centeredness.

3. 5-5-5 Breath

- Inhale for a count of 5
- Hold for a count of 5
- Exhale for a count of 5
- Repeat at least 5 times, or until you feel centered

Effect: Simple, easy to remember, and can be done anywhere. The number 5 is easy to recall, and the even rhythm creates a sense of safety.

Record your experience:

After trying these breathing techniques, record your experience. Which technique felt most natural? What changes did you notice in your body or mind?

....

....

....

....

....

....

....

....

....

....

....

....

....

....

ENDING WEEK 2: REFLECTION AND SUMMARY

Three things I've learned about the power of breath:

1. ....

....

2. ....

....

3. ....

....

A moment this week when breath helped me:

....

....

....

....

....

....

....

....

How I will continue to bring conscious breathing into my daily life:

....

....

....

....

....

....

....

A small intention I'm carrying into next week:

....

....

....

....

....

....

REMEMBER: *Like any skill, returning to the breath takes practice. Don't be discouraged if your mind wanders - that's its natural tendency. Each moment you notice you've disconnected and gently return to your breath is a moment of awakening and growth.*

YOUR WISE BODY

BREATH - THE GIFT ALWAYS PRESENT

IFor thousands of years, our bodies have developed a profound wisdom - a wisdom that far exceeds what the conscious mind perceives. When anxiety appears, the body is not just a container for uncomfortable sensations; it is also a teacher, a guide, and a repository of deep wisdom.

When we learn to listen to the body, we discover that many of the answers we seek already lie within. The body knows when we need rest, when we need movement, when something is wrong, and when we're heading in the right direction.

THE SCIENCE OF BODY WISDOM:

• Neuroscientist Antonio Damasio has demonstrated that bodily sensations (what he calls "somatic markers") play a decisive role in emotional and moral decision-making.

• Dr. Bessel van der Kolk, author of "The Body Keeps the Score," has described how the body stores emotional memories and trauma - and also holds the keys to healing.

• The enteric nervous system, often called the "second brain," contains about 100 million neurons and produces many neurotransmitters like serotonin - closely linked to our mood and emotions.

When we're anxious, the body often responds before the mind becomes aware. These sensations aren't "faults" or "malfunctions" - they are sophisticated information systems trying to communicate with us.

SELF-REGULATION WITH BODY WISDOM:

Below is a simple exercise to begin building a relationship with your body's wisdom. Practice when you're relatively calm, and then apply it when anxiety arises.

1. Find a comfortable space to sit or lie down.

2. Place one hand on your chest and one hand on your abdomen.

3. Close your eyes if that feels comfortable.

4. Begin to gently scan through different parts of your body, from the top of your head to your toes.

5. As you attend to each area, ask yourself: "Is there anything here that needs my attention?"

6. If you notice an area of tension or discomfort, breathe gently into that area.

7. Imagine that your breath is carrying warmth, light, or healing energy.

8. After scanning your entire body, thank your body's wisdom and gradually return to your normal state.

Record your experience:

After completing the exercise, write about your experience:

....

....

....

....

....

CONVERSING WITH YOUR BODY

One of the most powerful ways to access the body's wisdom is through dialogue. While it may seem strange to think about "talking" to your body, this practice has been used in many healing traditions and modern psychology.

DIALOGUE WITH THE BODY:

1. Find a quiet space where you won't be disturbed.

2. Begin by taking a few deep breaths, allowing your body to relax.

3. Place your attention on a specific part of your body that feels tense, uncomfortable, or simply draws your attention.

4. Imagine that this part of your body could speak to you. What would it say?

5. Then, imagine that you could respond. What would you ask it? What would you like to tell it?

6. Continue this dialogue, allowing it to unfold naturally.

Record the conversation:

[Space for drawing/writing]

Body:..............................

....

....

Me:...............................

....

....

Body:..............................

....

....

Me:......................................

....

....

Body:..................................

....

....

Me:......................................

....

....

Reflection:

What surprised you about this conversation?

....

....

....

What is your body trying to tell you through anxious sensations?

....

....

....

How might you respond to this need with compassion?

....

....

....

INNER EMBRACES

When anxiety overwhelms the nervous system, the body needs sooth-ing - just like a frightened child needs a comforting embrace. Physical self-soothing is a powerful way to activate our parasympathetic nervous system and create a sense of safety from within.

PHYSICAL SELF-SOOTHING TECHNIQUES:

1. Self-hug: Simple yet powerful, a self-hug activates pressure re-ceptors on the skin, helping release oxytocin and creating a sense of safety. Try crossing your arms in front of your chest, with each hand resting on the opposite shoulder.

2. Gentle holding: Place one hand on your heart and the other on your belly. Feel your heartbeat and breath beneath your palms.

3. Pressure point massage: Apply gentle pressure to points on the body:

- The area between your eyebrows

- The center of your chest

- The point below your collarbone (where the collarbone meets the sternum)

- The sides of your ribcage, just beneath the chest

4. Rhythmic touch: Gently pat or stroke your arms, the sides of your legs, or shoulders in rhythmic, mindful movements.

5. Weighted comfort: Hold a pillow, weighted blanket, or even a stuffed animal against your chest.

CREATE A SELF-SOOTHING "TOOLKIT":

Think about items that provide you with a sense of safety and com-fort. This might include:

- A special type of tea

- A favorite essential oil or perfume

- A soft scarf

• A small object you can hold in your hand (a smooth stone, crystal, or stress toy)

• Soothing music or soundsor stress toy)

List your self-soothing toolkit:

....

....

....

....

....

....

....

....

....

Self-soothing note for difficult moments:

Write a short note to yourself to read during anxious moments, reminding you of physical self-soothing techniques:

....

....

....

....

....

....

....

....

....

....

DAILY REFLECTION 1: THE BODY HOUSE

BODY METAPHOR:

The body is like a house—the only house you truly live in throughout your life. Each room contains different memories, sensations, and experiences. Sometimes, anxiety is like a strong wind blowing through the windows, shaking the walls. Other times, it's like a warning fire indicating that some part of the house needs attention. As you learn to listen to your house, you know exactly which room needs light, which needs warmth, and which needs repair.

Gentle prompt: Today my body needs...

....

....

....

One kind thing I did for my "house" today:

....

....

....

Connecting with the body: A moment today when I truly felt connected to my body was...

....

....

....

....

....

DAILY REFLECTION 2: THE BODY GARDEN

BODY METAPHOR:

The body is like a living garden——always growing, changing, and responding to how it's tended. Each sensation, each emotion, is like a different plant in the garden. Anxiety might be like weeds that grow quickly when we're not paying attention. But even weeds have their purpose——often to protect and warn. As we become careful gardeners, we learn to view everything that grows in our garden with curiosity and acceptance, knowing that each plant carries a message.

Gentle prompt: Today my body needs...

....

....

....

One kind thing I did for my "garden" today:

....

....

....

Tending the garden: If I listen to my body like a careful gardener, I might notice...

....

....

....

....

DAILY REFLECTION 3: THE BODY RIVER

BODY METAPHOR:

The body is like a river—always moving, always changing, yet always itself. Emotions and sensations flow through this river, sometimes as gentle currents, other times as powerful rapids. Anxiety might be like a rushing stream, but like all waters, it will eventually flow past. As we learn to swim with the current rather than against it, we find the natural rhythm and flow in our bodies.

Gentle prompt: Today my body needs...

....

....

....

One kind thing I did for my "river" today:

....

....

....

....

Flowing with sensations: When I allow feelings to flow through rather than resist them, I notice...

....

....

....

....

DAILY REFLECTION 4: THE BODY TREE

BODY METAPHOR:

The body is like a living tree—with deep roots, a steady trunk, and branches reaching outward. Just as trees must go through different seasons, our bodies also experience different periods of stress and recovery, growth and rest. Anxiety might be like strong winds shaking the branches, or warnings about an approaching winter. But like trees, our bodies have the wisdom to adjust, adapt and find balance again.

Gentle prompt: Today my body needs...

....

....

....

One kind thing I did for my "tree" today:

....

....

....

....

Rooting and reaching: When I imagine myself as a steady tree, I feel...

....

....

....

....

PHYSICAL NOURISHMENT FOR ANXIETY

Anxiety isn't just a mental state—it's profoundly and directly affected by our physical health. Here are some ways to nourish your body during times of anxiety.

NUTRITION FOR THE NERVOUS SYSTEM:

• **Nutrition for the nervous system** (found in fatty fish, flaxseeds, chia seeds) help support brain function and may reduce inflammation associated with anxiety.

• **Magnesium-rich foods** (like dark leafy greens, nuts, beans) help relax muscles and nerves.

• **Probiotic-rich foods** (like yogurt, kimchi, sauerkraut) enhance gut health, which is linked to mood and anxiety.

• **Anti-inflammatory foods** (like turmeric, ginger, green tea) can help reduce bodily stress.

• **High-quality protein** provides essential amino acids for neurotransmitter production.

THINGS TO AVOID OR REDUCE:

• **Caffeine** can exacerbate anxiety symptoms in many people.

• **Refined sugar** can cause spikes and then sharp drops in blood sugar, mimicking anxiety sensations.

• **Alcohol** though it may seem to soothe anxiety immediately, actually disrupts sleep and can worsen anxiety later.

• **Processed foods** often contain ingredients that can cause inflammation and affect mood.

MOVING WITH ANXIETY:

• **Gentle walking** especially in nature, can significantly reduce anxiety.

• **Gentle stretching exercises** help release muscle tension accumulated from anxiety.

- **Yoga and Tai Chi** combine movement with mindful breathing practices - a powerful combination for anxiety.

- **Any activity you truly enjoy** - because enjoyment in movement is key to sustainability.

REST AND RECOVERY:

- **Adequate sleep** is foundational to mental health; sleep deprivation significantly increases activation of the anxiety system.

- **Regular disconnection from technology** allows the nervous system to recover from constant stimulation.

- **Warm baths with Epsom salts** provide magnesium and help relax muscles.

- **Self-massage** or use a tennis ball or foam roller to soothe tension points.

REST AND RECOVERY:

Sleep is one of the most important factors in managing anxiety. Here are some healthy sleep habits:

- Establish a regular sleep schedule (even on weekends)
- Create a relaxing bedtime ritual
- Keep your bedroom cool, dark, and quiet
- Avoid screens at least an hour before bedtime
- Limit caffeine after noon
- Consider using white noise, sleep masks, or weighted blankets

Self-care for the anxious body:

Create a simple body care plan for yourself by choosing one or two ideas from each category above. Remember that consistency is key—small habits done regularly have more impact than large, infrequent efforts.

My body care plan:

....

....

....

....

....

....

....

....

....

....

....

....

....

....

....

....

....

....

....

....

ENDING WEEK 3: REFLECTION AND SUMMARY

Three things I've learned about my body's wisdom:

1. ....

....

2. ....

....

3. ....

....

A moment this week when I truly listened to my body:

....

....

....

....

....

....

....

....

How I will continue to honor and listen to my body:

....

....

....

....

....

....

....

....

A small intention I'm carrying into next week:

....

....

....

....

....

....

....

REMEMBER: *Your body is not the enemy in the battle with anxiety—it's your most valuable ally. As you learn to listen to, respect, and nourish it, your body becomes the place where you find peace, wisdom, and strength to face any challenge.*

WEEK 04
STANDING STRONG IN THE STORM

SKY AND CLOUDS

One of the most powerful metaphors in mindfulness practice is the image of the mind as the sky, and thoughts, emotions (including anxiety) as clouds passing through.

The sky is never harmed by clouds, whether they are dark storm clouds or light, wispy ones. The sky doesn't resist or cling to any cloud - it is simply the vast space that contains everything. Over time, every cloud, no matter how thick and dark, will move and pass on.

SKY AND CLOUDS PRACTICE:

1. Find a comfortable position to sit or lie down.

2. Close your eyes or lower your gaze.

3. Begin by noticing your breath, simply feeling it come in and go out.

4. Expand your awareness to include your entire experience - sounds, sensations, thoughts, emotions.

5. Imagine your mind as the vast, blue sky.

6. As thoughts, sensations, and emotions arise, view them as clouds drifting across the sky.

7. Rather than trying to change or push away any clouds (even the stormy clouds of anxiety), simply observe them passing through.

8. Remind yourself: "I am not my thoughts. I am not my anxiety. I am the vast sky, containing all of these experiences."

9. Practice for 5-10 minutes, or longer if you wish.

Reflect on your experience:

When observing thoughts and emotions pass by like clouds, what do you notice?

....

....

....

Are there any thoughts or emotions that tend to "stick" with you, harder to let go?

....

....

....

....

How does it feel to recognize that you are not your thoughts or emotions?

....

....

....

STEADY FEET

When anxiety makes us feel adrift, disconnected, or out of control, grounding techniques can help us return to the present moment and find a sense of stability and safety.

Grounding isn't a way to eliminate anxiety - it's a way for us to feel safe and present enough to face it. Like a tree with strong roots can stand firm through a storm, when we feel grounded, we can experience anxiety without being swept away by it.

THE STORY OF THE TREE:

There was an old oak tree that had stood firm for hundreds of years on a hilltop. One day, a young oak asked for the secret to surviving countless storms. The old tree replied: "The secret is not to fight against the wind, but to root more deeply. When the wind blows, I feel it, I move with it, but I remain standing because of my roots. The same applies to your life – storms will come, but if you stay deeply connected to the ground beneath you, you will not only survive but grow stronger after each storm."

QUICK GROUNDING TECHNIQUES:

Here are some grounding techniques you can use whenever you feel anxiety rising:

1. Feet grounding: Sitting or standing, place your feet flat on the floor. Notice the sensation of your feet contacting the ground. Imagine you're growing roots into the earth, connecting with the steadiness and stability of the earth.

2. Small object to hold: Hold a small object (like a pebble, crystal, coin, or even a key) in your hand. Notice how it feels - the weight, texture, temperature. When anxiety appears, grip the object to bring you back to the present moment.

3. The 5-4-3-2-1 principle:
- Sight: Identify 5 things you can see
- Touch: Feel 4 things you can touch
- Hearing: Notice 3 sounds you can hear
- Smell: Find 2 scents you can smell
- Taste: Recognize 1 taste you can experience

4. Grounding breath: Inhale deeply while counting to 4, hold your breath for a count of 2, exhale slowly counting to 6. While inhaling, imagine drawing stable energy up from the ground. While exhaling, imagine releasing anxiety and tension into the earth to be transformed.

5. Tapping both sides of the body: Gently tap alternating sides of your body (both arms, both legs, both shoulders) in a gentle rhythm. This is called "bilateral stimulation" and can help the brain process anxiety more effectively.

Create your personal grounding toolkit:

Use the space below to list objects, sensations, or techniques that help you feel grounded. This will be your personal toolkit you can use in moments of anxiety:

....

....

....

Grounding reminder:

Write a short sentence you can remind yourself of when feeling swept away by anxiety:

....

....

....

5-4-3-2-1: THE RETURN RITUAL

The 5-4-3-2-1 technique is one of the most powerful grounding tools, especially in moments of high anxiety. It brings you back to the present moment by engaging all your senses. Think of it as a ritual - a sacred way to bring yourself back to the present.

PRACTICE THE 5-4-3-2-1 RITUAL WITH ART

Instead of just listing things you notice, try adding a creative element to this ritual. In the spaces below, quickly draw or artistically describe what you notice:

5 THINGS YOU CAN SEE:

[Space for drawing/writing]

4 THINGS YOU CAN TOUCH:

[Space for drawing/writing]

3 THINGS YOU CAN HEAR:

[Space for drawing/writing]

2 THINGS YOU CAN SMELL:

[Space for drawing/writing]

1 THING YOU CAN TASTE:

[Space for drawing/writing]

Reflection:

How do you feel after completing this ritual?

....

....

....

What changes do you notice in your anxiety and in your sense of presence?

....

....

....

DAILY REFLECTION 1: STANDING FIRM AFTER THE STORM

A SHORT STORY ABOUT STANDING STRONG:

Sarah used to be terrified of thunderstorms. When lightning appeared, she would curl up, cover her ears and close her eyes, hoping it would end quickly. One day, while hiking, a sudden storm caught her by surprise. Too far to find shelter, she stood under a large tree canopy (not the safest idea, but the best option in the situation). As she stood there, soaking wet but safe, she decided to observe the storm rather than just fear it. She watched the lightning tear through the sky, she felt the earth shake with thunder, and gradually, awe began to replace fear. She still felt her heart racing, but now with excitement rather than terror. When the storm passed, she realized that she had not just survived - she had witnessed something beautiful and powerful. Sarah realized she could apply the same lesson to the "storms" of anxiety in her life. Rather than running away or resisting, sometimes just standing firm, observing, and letting it pass was enough.

Gentle prompt: What helped me stand firm today...

....

....

....

....

....

....

....

Reflection question: When I feel adrift, I find my ground by...

....

....

....

....

....

....

....

....

....

A moment of standing firm: Describe a situation when you felt anxious but found a way to ground yourself:

....

....

....

....

....

....

....

....

....

DAILY REFLECTION 2: THE LIGHTHOUSE IN THE STORM

A SHORT STORY ABOUT STANDING STRONG:

Miguel worked as a crisis coordinator, frequently facing stressful situations that required calm and full presence. In his early career years, he would often get swept up in the intense emotions of those around him. An older mentor taught him about the "inner lighthouse" - a quiet center within each of us that we can return to. "Lighthouses don't move from their position when storms come," the mentor explained. "They stand firm, shining even more powerfully during the darkest times." Miguel began practicing connecting with his inner presence during peaceful moments. When stressful situations arose, he would pause, breathe, and remind himself to return to that steady "lighthouse." This practice completely transformed how he responded to crisis - not by becoming numb, but by finding a solid place to stand while still deeply empathizing with others.

Gentle prompt: What helped me stand firm today...

....

....

....

....

....

....

....

....

Reflection question: When I feel adrift, I find my ground by...

....

....

....

....

....

....

....

....

....

....

My lighthouse: Describe or draw your "inner lighthouse" - the steady center you can return to when anxiety is strong:

....

....

....

....

....

....

....

....

....

....

DAILY REFLECTION 3: ROOTING LIKE AN ANCIENT TREE

A SHORT STORY ABOUT STANDING STRONG:

When Elena was diagnosed with an anxiety disorder, she felt as if her body had betrayed her. Panic attacks seemed to come from nowhere and take complete control of her life. In a therapy session, her therapist suggested she imagine herself as an ancient tree. "Ancient trees go through countless storms," the therapist explained. "They feel the wind, they move and bend, but they don't break because their roots go deep into the ground." Elena began practicing a simple meditation, imagining herself rooting deeply into the earth whenever she felt a panic attack forming. She focused on the sensation of her feet on the floor, or her body in the chair, and imagined invisible roots growing from her body, anchoring deep into the earth. What surprised her was that the panic attacks still came, but she was no longer as afraid of them as before. Like a tree standing in the wind, she could feel the fear blow through her without being overwhelmed by it.

Gentle prompt: What helped me stand firm today...

....

....

....

....

....

....

....

Reflection question: When I feel adrift, I find my ground by...

....

....

....

....

....

....

....

....

....

....

Rooting like an ancient tree: Imagine and describe your root system - the sources of strength, stability, and support in your life:

....

....

....

....

....

....

....

....

....

....

DAILY REFLECTION 4: THE ROCK IN THE STREAM

A SHORT STORY ABOUT STANDING STRONG:

At a meditation retreat, Aiden learned the metaphor of "the rock in the stream." The guide explained that our thoughts and emotions are like water flowing through a stream - constantly moving, changing, sometimes quiet, sometimes fierce. "When we get caught up in anxious thoughts, it's like we're swimming in the current, being carried away and sometimes drowning," the teacher explained. "But we can choose to become the rock - not stopping the flow, but steady while letting the water flow around us." Aiden began practicing this in daily life. When anxiety arose, instead of trying to stop it or being swept away by it, he imagined himself as the rock, observing anxious thoughts and emotions glide past around him. He was surprised to find that when he stopped fighting or running from anxiety, it lost much of its power and he could keep his feet on solid ground even amid strong emotions.

Gentle prompt: What helped me stand firm today...

....

....

....

....

....

....

....

....

....

....

Reflection question: When I feel adrift, I find my ground by...

....

....

....

....

....

....

....

....

....

....

My rock: Describe the qualities that help you become a steady "rock" in the stream of anxiety:

....

....

....

....

....

....

....

....

....

....

GROUNDING IN THE MOST DIFFICULT MOMENTS

Sometimes anxiety can be so overwhelming that ordinary grounding techniques seem insufficient. Below are some advanced techniques to use in extremely difficult moments:

1. Cold Water Technique: When anxiety becomes extreme, our nervous system can get stuck in a highly activated state. One way to abruptly shift this is to:

- Place your face in cold water for 30 seconds, or
- Place a cold cloth or ice pack on your face, especially the forehead and cheeks.
- Or hold an ice cube in your hand and focus on the cold sensation.

This triggers the "mammalian dive reflex" - a physiological response that slows the heart and activates your parasympathetic nervous system.

2. Extended 5-4-3-2-1 Technique: This is an expanded version of the basic 5-4-3-2-1 technique:

- 5 things you can see: Look at each detail closely - colors, textures, shapes, shadows, and light.
- 4 things you can touch: Really take time to feel each item - temperature, texture, moisture, weight.
- 3 things you can hear: Listen to sounds near and far - notice pitch, volume, rhythm.
- 2 things you can smell: Breathe deeply through your nose to notice scents in your space.
- 1 thing you can taste: Really focus on the taste - salty, sweet, sour, bitter, umami.

Spend at least 30 seconds on each sense and describe your experience in detail either mentally or out loud if possible.

3. Grounding Pad: Create a "grounding pad" that you can carry with you. This could be:

- A small card with a list of places, people, and moments where you felt safe
- A photograph or small object that reminds you of a place where you felt peaceful
- A piece of fabric with a familiar and comforting scent

In moments of intense anxiety, take out your pad and interact with it using all your senses.

4. Counting and Moving Technique: The combination of physical movement and mental focus can be particularly powerful:

- Count backward from 100 in steps of 7 (100, 93, 86...)
- While counting, perform a simple but slightly attention-demanding body movement (such as walking in a figure 8 pattern, or touching your thumb to each finger in order)

The combination of mental challenge and physical movement helps pull the mind out of the anxiety spiral.

5. Sensory Grounding: Prepare a "grounding kit" with items that impact each sense:

- Visual: A beautiful picture or a slideshow on your phone of favorite people/places
- Tactile: A piece of soft fabric, a smooth stone, or something that provides mild sensory stimulation like a clickable pen
- Auditory: A specific song or sound (ocean waves, rainfall) ready on your phone
- Olfactory: A familiar scent (essential oil, cinnamon, mint)
- Taste: A mint, raisin, or special tea

Create your personal grounding plan for the most difficult moments:

ENDING WEEK 4: REFLECTION AND SUMMARY

Three grounding techniques that worked best for me:

1. ....

....

2. ....

....

3. ....

....

A moment this week when I practiced grounding:

....

....

....

....

....

....

....

....

Changes I've noticed after practicing grounding techniques:

....

....

....

....

....

....

....

A small intention I'm carrying into next week:

....

....

....

....

....

....

....

REMEMBER: *Standing strong isn't about never feeling anxious, but finding enough safety and presence to experience whatever arises. Like an ancient tree in a storm, you can feel the wind and move with it, while remaining standing because of your roots.*

LISTENING TO INNER VOICES

THE STORIES WE TELL OURSELVES

Inside each of us is a constant storyteller - an inner voice continuously interpreting what's happening in our lives and creating meaning from our experiences. When anxiety appears, this storyteller often tells fearful, catastrophic stories about the worst things that could happen.

We can't completely turn off this inner voice, but we can learn to recognize it, understand its patterns, and gradually recreate the stories we tell ourselves.

EXPLORING YOUR INNER STORIES:

First, let's explore what your inner storyteller typically says about anxiety-provoking situations. In the space below, record some familiar stories your mind tends to tell about:

1. Yourself:

....

....

....

....

....

....

2. Your abilities:

....

....

....

....

3. The future:

....

....

....

....

4. How others perceive you:

....

....

....

....

....

5. A specific situation that's causing you anxiety right now:

....

....

....

....

....

....

IDENTIFYING PATTERNS IN YOUR STORIES:

Below are some common thought patterns that might appear in our inner narratives:

- **Catastrophizing:** Imagining the worst-case scenario will happen

- **Mind reading:** Assuming you know what others are thinking (usually something negative)

- **Binary thinking:** Seeing things as only right/wrong, good/bad with no nuance in between

- **Magnifying weaknesses:** Exaggerating your weaknesses and minimizing your strengths

- **Personalizing:** Assuming everything is about you

- **Looking through a dark lens:** Only focusing on the negative aspects of situations

Based on what you wrote above, which patterns can you recognize in your stories?

....

....

....

....

....

....

....

....

REWRITING YOUR STORY:

Choose one of the stories you identified above and rewrite it from a different perspective - one that is more balanced, compassionate, and realistic:

Original story:

....

....

....

....

....

Rewritten story:

....

....

....

....

....

....

THE VOICE OF FEAR

Each of us has an "inner critic" - a part of our mind that acts as a monitor, evaluator, and frequent judge of ourselves. For many people, this voice is particularly active when anxiety appears.

This inner critic is often not the enemy we think it is. It's usually a part of us trying to protect - perhaps by preparing for the worst, trying to make us perfect to avoid rejection, or keeping us vigilant for danger.

IDENTIFYING YOUR INNER CRITIC:

Imagine your inner critic as a character. What does it look like? How does it speak? When does it appear most often? Describe or draw it in the space below:

[Space for drawing/writing]

WRITE A LETTER IN RESPONSE:

Now, write a letter back to your inner critic. Remember that the goal isn't to defeat or silence it, but to understand and interact with it in a more supportive way.

Dear my inner critic

....

....

....

....

....

LISTENING TO THE HEART SPEAK

Besides the inner critic, we have another voice inside - the voice of the heart, of compassion. This is the voice that understands, supports, and empathizes.

When anxiety is present, the voice of the heart is often drowned out by the shouting of fear. But with practice, we can learn to listen to this gentler voice and allow it to guide us.

FINDING YOUR HEART'S VOICE:

Close your eyes and imagine someone you love experiencing the exact anxiety you're feeling. What would you say to them? How would you treat them? Write down the words you would say:

....

....

....

....

....

Now, imagine saying these words to yourself. How does it feel to receive this gentleness and understanding?

....

....

....

....

....

....

DEVELOPING YOUR COMPASSIONATE VOICE:

Below are some heart-centered phrases you can customize and use when anxiety appears:

1. "I understand you're going through a difficult time. I'm here with you."

2. "This feeling will pass. You are safe."

3. "You don't need to be perfect. You're doing the best you can."

4. "You're not alone. Many people experience similar feelings."

5. "Whatever happens, we'll get through it together."

Write 3-5 heart centered phrases you can use during anxious moments:

....

....

....

....

....

PRACTICING BOTH/AND THINKING:

When anxiety appears, the critical mind and the compassionate heart often conflict with each other. Instead of letting one voice win, try practicing "Both/And" dialogue:

Example:

• Anxious mind: "I'm going to mess up this presentation and everyone will think I'm incompetent."

• Both/And dialogue: "I both feel anxious about the presentation AND know that I've prepared thoroughly and have valuable things to share."

Try an example from your own life:

Anxious mind:...

....

....

....

....

....

....

....

....

....

Both/And dialogue:..

....

....

....

....

....

....

....

....

DAILY REFLECTION 1: TWO VOICES

Situation: Receiving an email from your boss saying "We need to talk tomorrow."

The voice of anxiety says: "Oh no, I'm about to get fired. I must have done something wrong. It's probably that project last week - I knew I should have spent more time on it. Now I won't be able to find another job in this economy, and I'll disappoint my family..."

But my heart knows: "This could be about many different things. My boss often wants to discuss new projects at the beginning of the week. Even if there is an issue to address, it doesn't mean disaster. I'm capable of handling difficult conversations and finding solutions. Whatever happens, I'll face it with the same dedication and courage I've shown before."

Gentle prompt: The voice of anxiety tells me...

....

....

....

....

....

....

....

....

....

But my heart knows...

....

....

....

....

....

....

....

....

....

One way I can nurture the voice of my heart today:

....

....

....

....

....

....

....

....

....

....

DAILY REFLECTION 2: OLD STORIES AND NEW STORIES

SITUATION AND TWO VOICES:

Situation: Preparing to attend a social event where you'll meet many new people.

The voice of anxiety says: "I always become awkward and weird in social situations. I'll say something stupid and people will judge me. It's best to avoid talking much. Actually, maybe I should find a way not to attend."

But my heart knows: "Meeting new people can be stressful for anyone. My experience at previous events has actually been quite successful - I've had interesting conversations and even made new friends. Even when I feel uncomfortable, it doesn't mean I'm coming across poorly. I can feel anxious AND still connect with others in meaningful ways."

Gentle prompt: The voice of anxiety tells me...

....

....

....

....

....

....

....

....

....

....

But my heart knows...

....

....

....

....

....

....

....

....

....

A story I tell myself that I want to change:

....

....

....

....

....

....

....

....

....

....

DAILY REFLECTION 3: WHISPERS OF FEAR

Situation: Having to make an important decision about changing jobs or where to live.

The voice of anxiety says: "This is too big a decision. What if I choose wrong? I could ruin my future with one wrong choice. Maybe I should just stay where I am, even if I'm not that happy. At least I know how to deal with the current problems."

But my heart knows: "No decision is perfect, and most decisions aren't permanent. Change is always scary, but it also brings opportunities for growth. I have the wisdom and resilience to navigate whatever comes. Many paths can lead to a good life, and I can trust my intuition to guide me."

Gentle prompt: The voice of anxiety tells me...

....

....

....

....

....

....

....

....

....

....

But my heart knows...

....

....

....

....

....

....

....

....

....

If I listen to my heart about this situation, I would...

....

....

....

....

....

....

....

....

....

DAILY REFLECTION 4: DIALOGUE WITH FEAR

SITUATION AND TWO VOICES:

Situation: Feeling worried about your health after noticing an unusual symptom.

The voice of anxiety says: "This could be a sign of a serious illness. Why can't the doctor see me sooner? I should look online to see what this could be. Oh no, there are so many bad possibilities. I always had a feeling something terrible would happen."

But my heart knows: "My body often has strange sensations that are mostly harmless. Worry can actually make physical symptoms worse. I've scheduled a doctor's appointment, which is the responsible action. Until then, I can take care of myself by focusing on things that bring peace and wellness. Whatever happens, I have the capacity to face it."

Gentle prompt: The voice of anxiety tells me...

....

....

....

....

....

....

....

....

....

....

But my heart knows...

....

....

....

....

....

....

....

....

....

A way to balance between reasonable concern and excessive anxiety:

....

....

....

....

....

....

....

....

....

....

....

TRANSFORMATIVE QUESTIONS FOR ANXIETY

When anxiety is strong, the questions we ask ourselves can have a major impact on our experience. Some questions can lead us deeper into the anxiety spiral, while others can open up space for understanding, acceptance, and change.

FROM CLOSED QUESTIONS TO OPEN QUESTIONS:

Instead of asking: "Why am I so anxious?" Try asking: "What is needing my attention right now?"

Instead of asking: "How can I get rid of this feeling?" Try asking: "How might I be present with this feeling in a gentler way?"

Instead of asking: "What if things go wrong?" Try asking: "What will support me no matter what happens?"

CREATE YOUR OWN TRANSFORMATIVE QUESTIONS:

Identify three questions that your anxious mind typically asks, and then create an alternative question that helps open up understanding and compassion:

Anxiety question 1:..Transformative question:........

....

Anxiety question 2: .... Transformative question: ....

....

Anxiety question 3: .... Transformative question: ....

....

INQUIRY PRACTICE:

The most powerful question when facing anxious thoughts is some-times the simplest. Practice gently asking: "Is this really true?"

Identify an anxious thought you frequently have:

....

....

....

....

Now ask: "Is this really true?" and write what emerges:

....

....

....

....

Then ask: "How do I know this is absolutely true?"

....

....

....

....

....

Finally ask: "Who would I be without this thought?"

....

....

....

....

....

ENDING WEEK 5: REFLECTION AND SUMMARY

Three things I've learned about my inner voices:

1. ....
....

2. ....
....

3. ....
....

How the voice of anxiety and the voice of the heart differ:

....
....
....
....
....
....
....
....

A story I tell myself that I'm beginning to change:

....
....
....
....
....
....
....

A small intention I'm carrying into next week:

....
....
....
....
....
....
....

REMEMBER: *You are not the voice of anxiety, and you don't need to believe everything it says. By learning to recognize, listen to, and respond to your inner stories with compassion, you begin to change your relationship with anxiety. This change doesn't happen overnight, but each moment of awareness is a step forward on the journey.*

THE CIRCLE OF TOLERANCE

Each of us has a "window of tolerance" - an emotional range that we can comfortably handle. Within this window, we can think clearly, regulate our emotions, and connect with others. When anxiety becomes intense, we're often pushed outside this window - either into a state of overwhelm or shutdown.

The good news is: we can expand this window of tolerance over time and practice. Rather than being knocked over by strong emotions, we can develop the capacity to contain more while remaining in balance.

THE STORY OF THE WINDOW OF TOLERANCE:

Imagine your mind as a house with windows. When the windows are open moderately, warmth and light can come in, but you're still protected from rain and harsh weather. But when an anxiety storm appears, strong winds can push the windows too wide open, causing everything inside to be blown around and disrupted (overwhelm). Or, overwhelmed by the storm's power, you might slam the windows shut and lock the doors, making the house dark and isolated (shutdown).

Over time, with practice and patience, you can build a more sturdy window, with stronger hinges that can open wider without being blown away, and with smoother mechanisms so you can adjust as needed. You can also develop the ability to repair your window when it's damaged by particularly strong storms. This is how we expand our circle of tolerance.

RECOGNIZING THE SIGNS:

It's important to recognize when you're inside or outside your window of tolerance. Consider your personal signs:

Signs I'm in my window of tolerance (feeling balanced, flexible):

....

....

....

....

....

Signs I'm in a state of overwhelm (high, tense, angry, anxious):

....

....

....

....

....

Signs I'm in a state of shutdown (low, empty, isolated, numb):

....

....

....

....

....

....

EXPANDING YOUR CIRCLE OF TOLERANCE:

Below are some ways to expand your window of tolerance, creating more space for anxious feelings and experiences without becoming overwhelmed:

1. Build body awareness: Practice noticing sensations in your body before they become too intense. This helps you recognize when you're approaching the edge of your window of tolerance.

2. Regulate your nervous system: Use techniques like deep breathing, rhythmic movement, and feeling the ground beneath you to bring your nervous system back into balance.

3. Develop internal resources: Identify and nurture inner resources (like patience, courage, calmness) that you can draw upon when anxiety rises.

4. Create observer space: Practice the ability to "witness" your anxious experience rather than being engulfed by it, creating space between you and intense feelings.

EXPANDING YOUR CIRCLE OF TOLERANCE:

The next time you feel anxiety arising, try practicing these steps:

1. Notice: "I'm feeling anxious" (name the experience)

2. ULocate where in your body you feel it

3. Imagine creating space around that sensation

4. Breathe in, imagining the space around the sensation expanding

5. Breathe out, allowing your body to relax into that space

6. Remind yourself: "I am larger than this feeling. I can contain it."

After practicing, record your experience::

....

....

....

....

CREATING SPACE FOR EMOTIONS

One of the most common reactions to uncomfortable emotions like anxiety is trying to avoid, suppress, or control them. However, these strategies often make emotions stronger in the long run.

Instead, we can learn to "make space" for emotions - an approach that may seem counterintuitive at first, but brings freedom and flexibility over time.

EXERCISE: EMOTIONAL WAVES

1. Close your eyes or lower your gaze, and take a few deep breaths.

2. Bring attention to any anxious feelings that are present, whether small or large.

3. Imagine this emotion as a wave in the ocean of your consciousness:

   • Notice where the wave begins

   • Observe it as it rises

   • Feel it as it reaches its peak

   • Watch it as it gradually subsides

4. Remind yourself that like all waves, this emotion will naturally pass if you don't resist it.

5. Repeat with any new emotional waves that arise.

Write about your experience:

....

....

....

....

....

....

....

....

EXERCISE: EXPANDING EMOTIONAL SPACE

This is a powerful exercise to practice when you notice yourself resisting anxious feelings:

1. Notice and name: "I'm feeling anxious" (or whatever specific emotion is present).

2. Locate: Where in your body does this emotion appear? Does it have a shape, size, weight, or temperature?

3. Create space: Imagine you're expanding the space inside yourself, making more room for this emotion to exist. Imagine you're creating space between yourself and the emotion.

4. Accept presence: Rather than trying to change the emotion, simply acknowledge: "This is what's happening right now, and I can make space for it in my awareness."

5. Repeat key statement: "I am not this anxiety. I am the space that contains it."

BASIC INSTRUCTIONS FOR YOURSELF:

Write down a few short sentences to remind yourself how to create space for uncomfortable emotions:

....

....

....

....

OBSERVING INSTEAD OF ESCAPING

When anxiety appears, our natural instinct is often to try to escape the uncomfortable feeling as quickly as possible. However, there's another approach that many mindfulness traditions and modern therapeutic methods suggest: turning toward anxiety, observing it with curiosity and non-judgment.

EXERCISE: FACING ANXIOUS SENSATIONS

This is an exercise to practice when you notice anxious feelings arising:

1. When you feel anxiety beginning to appear, rather than trying to escape it, try **turning toward it**.

2. Imagine that you're rotating your chair 180 degrees to directly face the anxiety.

3. With genuine curiosity, ask yourself:

- What does this sensation look like?

- Does it have a taste, texture, or temperature?

- How does it change as I pay attention to it?

- What might it be trying to tell me?

4. Imagine you're making space for the anxiety to be present, without trying to change, fix, or eliminate it.

5. Remind yourself: "I don't need to like this feeling. I just need to make space for it to exist."

Write about your experience:

....

....

....

....

....

....

EXERCISE: APPLYING CURIOSITY TO ANXIETY

When we approach anxiety with genuine curiosity, it often changes our experience. Here's an exercise to develop a curious perspective:

1. Recall a recent moment when you felt anxious.

2. Imagine you're a scientist studying this anxiety phenomenon with professional detachment and curiosity.

3. Write down your observations about:

- The first signs that anxiety was about to appear

- How it developed in the body

- The thoughts that accompanied it

- The behaviors it triggered

- How it gradually decreased and ended

4. What helped soothe it? What made it worse?

5. If you could ask your anxiety one question, what would it be?

Observation notes:

....

....

....

....

....

....

....

....

....

....

....

....

....

....

....

....

....

....

DAILY REFLECTION 1:
SPACE FOR SMALL THINGS

A VISUALIZATION ABOUT EXPANDING SPACE:

Imagine your mind as the vast, blue sky. In this infinite space, anxious thoughts and feelings are like clouds - whatever shape or size, they cannot fill or limit the sky. Sometimes, the clouds may become thick, forming fierce storms, and may block your entire view. But above those clouds, the sky remains clear, open, and unlimited. You are not the clouds - you are the sky that contains them.

Gentle prompt: Today I created space for...

....

....

....

....

....

....

....

....

....

....

....

....

....

Reflection question: When I don't resist, I notice...

....

....

....

....

....

....

....

....

....

Expanding space for a specific situation: Identify a small anxiety-provoking situation. Write about how you might create more space to deal with it:

....

....

....

....

....

....

....

....

....

DAILY REFLECTION 2:
SPACE FOR BIG CHALLENGES

A VISUALIZATION ABOUT EXPANDING SPACE:

Imagine your heart as a room with the ability to expand infinitely. When strong emotions appear - whether fear, anxiety, or sadness - the room automatically expands to contain them. No need to push anything out, no need to compress or force. Just the space expanding, making more room. In this expanded space, even the most intense emotions can move freely, change, and eventually find their own balance. Your heart is big enough to hold everything.

Gentle prompt: Today I created space for...

....

....

....

....

....

....

....

....

....

....

....

....

Reflection question: When I don't resist, I notice...

....

....

....

....

....

....

....

....

....

Expanding space for a major challenge: Identify a larger challenge causing anxiety. Write about how you might apply the principle of creating space:

....

....

....

....

....

....

....

....

....

....

DAILY REFLECTION 3: SPACE IN RELATIONSHIPS

A VISUALIZATION ABOUT EXPANDING SPACE:

Imagine the space between you and others as a wide-open stage. In this space, both joy and conflict can be present; both connection and misunderstanding have room. Imagine this space is wide enough to hold both your emotions and the emotions of others, without either person having to shrink for the other to have room. With this expanded space, difficult conversations can unfold with calmness and mutual respect, strong emotions can be expressed without overwhelming, and both parties can feel heard and seen.

Gentle prompt: Today I created space for...

....

....

....

....

....

....

....

....

....

....

....

....

Reflection question: When I don't resist, I notice...

....

....

....

....

....

....

....

....

Expanding space in relationships: Identify a relationship that causes anxiety. Write about how you might create more space in interaction:

....

....

....

....

....

....

....

....

....

DAILY REFLECTION 4: SPACE FOR UNCERTAINTY

A VISUALIZATION ABOUT EXPANDING SPACE:

Imagine your mind as a vast garden, where everything is in the process of growing and changing. Some areas are carefully planned, while others are left to grow naturally. There are clear paths leading through the garden, but also unexplored spaces, plots of land still open. Uncertainty, like seeds not yet sprouted, is welcomed in this garden. You don't need to know how everything will develop. The joy is in creating space for surprise, for the unknown, and for possibilities not yet explored.

Gentle prompt: Today I created space for...

....

....

....

....

....

....

....

....

....

....

....

....

Reflection question: When I don't resist, I notice...

....

....

....

....

....

....

....

....

....

Expanding space for uncertainty: Identify an uncertain situation causing anxiety. Write about how you might create more space for this uncertainty:

....

....

....

....

....

....

....

....

....

Expanding your circle of tolerance doesn't happen overnight, but is a gradual process that unfolds over time. Below are some specific ways to continue building your capacity to contain more emotions and experiences without becoming overwhelmed.

1. Practice "window of tolerance" daily:

• **When feeling calm:** Actively seek out comfortable and uncomfortable sensations at mild levels to expand what you can tolerate. For example: taste new foods, experience slightly cold or warm temperatures, or engage in mild social situations that require you to step outside your comfort zone.

• **When feeling anxious:** Practice staying with the feeling, creating space for it, and recognizing when you're approaching the edge of your window of tolerance. The goal isn't to push past the edge, but to gradually expand the boundaries.

2. Build a regulation toolkit:

Create a list of activities that help bring you back into your circle of tolerance when you feel yourself falling out. This list might include:

• **When feeling overwhelmed (high state):** Calming activities like deep breathing, hugging a pillow, taking a warm bath, lying under a weighted blanket, listening to gentle music, foot pressure points.

• **When feeling shut down (low state):** Gentle activating activities like a short walk, stretching, washing your face with cool water, eating something mildly spicy or sour, listening to upbeat music.

Write your toolkit list:

To handle feeling overwhelmed:

....

....

....

....

....

....

....

....

....

To handle feeling shut down:

....

....

....

....

....

....

....

....

....

3. Daily practices to expand capacity:

Choose one or two exercises from the following list to practice daily, rotating between exercises over weeks:

- **Box Breathing Practice:** 4 seconds inhale, 4 seconds hold, 4 seconds exhale, 4 seconds hold. Repeat 4-8 times.

- **Emotions in the Body:** Notice any emotions that arise during the day and locate exactly where they sit in your body. Create space for them without trying to change them.

- **Thought Watching:** Spend 5-10 minutes simply observing thoughts come and go, without judging or attaching to them.

- **Emotion Blocks:** When strong emotions arise, imagine them as physical blocks. What size, shape, color, weight, and texture do they have? Observe how they change as you pay attention to them.

- **"Both/And" Practice:** Notice when you fall into binary thinking (good/bad, right/wrong) and practice shifting to "both/and" thinking. For example: "I both feel nervous about this meeting AND know that I have valuable things to contribute."

TRACK YOUR PROGRESS:

Monitor how you're building capacity over time. How is your circle of tolerance today compared to last week?

....

....

....

....

....

ENDING WEEK 6: REFLECTION AND SUMMARY

Three things I've learned about creating space:

1. ....

....

2. ....

....

3. ....

....

A moment this week when I created space for my experience instead of resisting it:

....

....

....

....

....

....

....

How I notice my circle of tolerance changing:

....

....

....

....

....

....

....

....

A small intention I'm carrying into next week:

....

....

....

....

....

....

REMEMBER: *Each time you practice creating space for uncomfortable emotions rather than resisting them, you're expanding your capacity for tolerance. This doesn't mean you have to like those emotions, just that you're learning to be with them without being overwhelmed. Over time, this capacity creates a deeper sense of freedom and flexibility in dealing with anxiety.*

SMALL BRAVE STEPS

COURAGE IS NOT THE ABSENCE OF FEAR

Many of us think of courage as a state without fear - heroes in movies seem to act without hesitation or worry. But in reality, true courage is not the absence of fear. Rather, it's the ability to move forward, to take actions aligned with our values, even while feelings of fear are present.

This is good news: you don't need to wait until anxiety disappears before you can begin building a meaningful life. You can feel anxious AND simultaneously take courageous steps.

A STORY ABOUT COURAGE:

An ancient tale tells of a young warrior preparing for his first battle. The young man had trained for many years, but as the day of departure drew near, fear began to flood his soul. Feeling ashamed of his fear, he visited his elderly teacher.

"Master," he said, "I fear I don't have courage. My heart trembles when I think of battle."

The teacher smiled and asked, "Do you think the greatest warriors feel no fear?"

"I suppose so," the young man replied.

"Then look at our army as they prepare for battle. Look at their hands."

The next day, the young man observed the experienced warriors. He was surprised to see that their hands also trembled, just like his.

When he returned to his teacher, he asked, "But if they are also afraid, how did they become great warriors?"

"True courage is not about feeling no fear," the teacher explained. "It's about the ability to act wisely even when you are afraid. This is what makes them great - not that they never tremble, but that they move forward even when their hands shake."

REFLECTING ON COURAGE:

Think about someone you consider courageous. What makes them courageous in your eyes? Are they completely fearless, or do they act despite fear?

....

....

....

....

When have you acted with courage in the past, even while feeling anxious or afraid?

....

....

....

REDEFINING COURAGE:

Write your own definition of courage, one that allows both fear and brave action to coexist:

....

....

....

DANCING WITH FEAR

When facing anxiety, many of us tend to either completely avoid frightening situations, or try to force ourselves to face them too quickly, leading to overwhelm. Both approaches can make anxiety stronger.

Instead, we can learn to "dance" with fear - approaching it with fluidity, knowing when to step forward and when to step back. This is a gradual, gentle approach to facing anxiety-provoking situations.

EXERCISE: DANCING WITH FEAR

Imagine your fear as a dance partner. As you approach your comfort boundary, fear might lead for a while. When you become too anxious, you step back a bit and take the lead. It's a dance, not a battle - and over time, you become more comfortable with the steps.

1. Choose a moderately anxiety-provoking situation (not too overwhelming).

2. Approach this situation slowly and intentionally.

3. Notice the anxious sensations that arise in your body.

4. Stay with these sensations while practicing grounding techniques (breathing, naming emotions, etc.).

5. If anxiety rises too high, step back a bit - take a small self-care action.

6. When ready, approach the situation again.

7. Continue this dance, gradually moving closer to what scares you.

EXERCISE: DANCING WITH FEAR

Describe an anxiety-provoking situation you've "danced" with this week:

....

....

....

Describe an anxiety-provoking situation you've "danced" with this week:

....

....

....

How did you feel during this process?

....

....

....

What did you learn about yourself and your anxiety?

....

....

....

FEAR LADDER

One of the most effective techniques for facing anxiety is creating a "fear ladder" - a list of situations related to your specific fear, arranged from least to most frightening. By facing these situations step by step, from easier to harder, you gradually build confidence and expand your tolerance for anxiety.

BUILDING A FEAR LADDER:

1. Identify a specific area that causes anxiety (e.g., public speaking, flying, relationship conflicts, etc.).

2. List 8-10 situations related to this area, arranged from least anxiety-provoking to most anxiety-provoking. Each "rung" should be slightly more challenging than the previous one, but not so difficult that you would completely avoid it.

3. Beside each rung, rate the expected anxiety level from 0-10 (0 = no anxiety, 10 = extreme anxiety).

4. Start with the lowest rung. Repeat exposure to this situation until your anxiety level decreases to about half of your initial rating. Then move to the next rung.

5. For each rung, prepare coping strategies (deep breathing, creating space for emotions, compassionate reminders, etc.) to use during exposure.

HERE'S AN EXAMPLE OF A FEAR LADDER FOR SOCIAL ANXIETY:

Rung 1: Smile at a stranger in a store (Anxiety level: 3/10) Rung 2: Ask a store employee a simple question (4/10) Rung 3: Start a brief conversation with a coworker (5/10) Rung 4: Speak up with your opinion in a small meeting (6/10) Rung 5: Have lunch with a group of colleagues (6/10) Rung 6: Call an acquaintance you haven't spoken to in a while (7/10) Rung 7: Attend a social event where you know only one or two people (8/10) Rung 8: Give a short presentation to a small group (9/10) Rung 9: Attend an event alone and actively make new friends (9/10) Rung 10: Speak in front of a large crowd (10/10)

CREATE YOUR FEAR LADDER:

Anxiety-provoking area: ....

Rung 1: .... (Anxiety level: __/10)

Rung 2: .... (Anxiety level: __/10)

Rung 3: .... (Anxiety level: __/10)

Rung 4: .... (Anxiety level: __/10)

Rung 5: .... (Anxiety level: __/10)

Rung 6: .... (Anxiety level: __/10)

Rung 7: .... (Anxiety level: __/10)

Rung 8: .... (Anxiety level: __/10)

Rung 9: .... (Anxiety level: __/10)

Rung 10: .... (Anxiety level: __/10)

STRATEGIES TO SUPPORT YOU WHILE CLIMBING THE LADDER:

....

....

....

....

....

....

....

....

....

PROGRESS NOTES:

Which rung are you currently working on? ....

What changes have you noticed when repeating exposure to
this situation?

....

....

....

....

....

....

....

....

....

DAILY REFLECTION 1: A SMALL BRAVE STEP

A SHORT STORY ABOUT EVERYDAY COURAGE:

Maria had been anxious about making phone calls since she was young. Whenever she needed to call someone - whether it was a restaurant to make a reservation, a doctor to make an appointment, or even close friends - her heart would pound and her hands would shake. Usually, she would avoid it and send a text or email instead.

One day, Maria needed to call to arrange an important interview for her dream job. There was no other way. Instead of letting anxiety control her, she decided to take a small step. First, she wrote down what she needed to say. Then she practiced deep breathing. Finally, she reminded herself that the call would only last a few minutes.

When Maria finally made the call, still feeling anxious, she realized something: she could feel afraid AND still accomplish what needed to be done. The call wasn't perfect - her voice shook a bit and she forgot to ask one question - but she did it. And with each subsequent call, though still anxious, she found herself becoming a bit more confident.

Gentle prompt: A small step I tried today...

....

....

....

....

....

....

....

Reflection question: What I learned about myself when facing...

....

....

....

....

....

....

....

....

....

Next step: A small step I want to try tomorrow is...

....

....

....

....

....

....

....

....

....

....

DAILY REFLECTION 2: COURAGE IN THE MOMENT

A SHORT STORY ABOUT EVERYDAY COURAGE:

James always found it difficult to say "no" to others. Afraid of disappointing people, he would agree to requests even when they left him overwhelmed and stressed. Each time the pressure mounted, his anxiety increased, affecting his sleep and overall wellbeing.

One day, a colleague asked James to help with a project over the weekend - when he already had important plans with family. As usual, anxiety rushed in, urging him to agree. But this time, James decided to try something different. He took a deep breath, acknowledged his fear, and gently said, "I'm sorry, but I can't this weekend. I have important family plans."

James' heart pounded as he said these words, but something surprising happened: his colleague simply said "No problem, I'll ask someone else." And that was it. No one was angry. No one was disappointed. In that moment, James realized that sometimes the greatest courage lies in the smallest actions - like setting healthy boundaries even when you feel afraid.

Gentle prompt: A small step I tried today...

....

....

....

....

....

....

....

....

Reflection question: What I learned about myself when facing...

....

....

....

....

....

....

....

....

....

Moment of courage: A moment today when I felt anxious but moved forward anyway:

....

....

....

....

....

....

....

....

....

....

DAILY REFLECTION 3: THE POWER OF SMALL ACTIONS

A SHORT STORY ABOUT EVERYDAY COURAGE:

Emily had struggled with anxiety disorder for years. One of her biggest fears was riding public buses. The feeling of being trapped, the noise, and the proximity to strangers would often trigger panic attacks. As a result, her world became increasingly small as she avoided traveling beyond walking distance.

When a good job opportunity appeared on the other side of town, Emily knew she needed to expand her world. Rather than trying to ride a bus during rush hour immediately (which would overwhelm her), she started with an extremely small step: one Sunday, she walked to the bus stop just to look at the schedule. The next day, she went to the stop and waited for a bus to arrive, but didn't get on. On the third try, she boarded a nearly empty bus and rode for just one stop before getting off.

Gradually, with each small step, Emily's world began to expand again. She still felt anxious when riding buses, but each small brave action built her confidence and capacity. What she learned wasn't how to eliminate anxiety completely, but how to live a full life even while anxiety was present.

Gentle prompt: A small step I tried today...

....

....

....

....

....

....

....

Reflection question: What I learned about myself when facing...

....

....

....

....

....

....

....

....

....

Plan for small steps: A sequence of small steps I could take to face a challenge:

....

....

....

....

....

....

....

....

....

....

DAILY REFLECTION 4: COURAGE IN SELF-CARE

A SHORT STORY ABOUT EVERYDAY COURAGE:

Thomas had always been the caretaker - the person friends and family turned to when they needed help. He was always ready to put his own needs aside to support others. This gave him a sense of value, but it also left him exhausted and anxious as he tried to please everyone.

When Thomas' mental health began to decline, his therapist suggested a surprising idea: perhaps the most courageous act sometimes is to prioritize your own needs. To Thomas, this seemed selfish and frightening. If he wasn't always available for others, would they still need him?

Thomas started with a small step - spending 30 minutes each day doing something just for himself without feeling guilty. At first, it was a challenge. Anxiety and guilt kept creeping in. But gradually, he realized that when he prioritized his own needs, he actually had more to give. He was no longer operating from a place of constant depletion.

Sometimes, the bravest lesson is realizing that self-care isn't selfish - it's a necessary foundation for being truly present for others and for yourself.

Gentle prompt: A small step I tried today...

....

....

....

....

....

....

....

Reflection question: What I learned about myself when facing...

....

....

....

....

....

....

....

....

....

Brave self-care action: One way that self-care requires courage for me is.

....

....

....

....

....

....

....

....

....

....

....

THE 5-4-3-2-1 RULE FOR COURAGEOUS ACTION

When facing anxiety about a challenge or brave step you need to take, use the 5-4-3-2-1 rule to help you move from worry to action:

5: ACKNOWLEDGE 5 ANXIOUS THOUGHTS YOU HAVE

List 5 anxious thoughts you have about the specific action/situation. Just recognize them without judgment:

1. ....

2. ....

3. ....

4. ....

5. ....

4: IDENTIFY 4 WORST THINGS THAT COULD HAPPEN

List 4 actual worst-case scenarios. This is a way to face your fears directly:

1. ....

2. ....

3. ....

4. ....

3: LIST 3 COPING RESOURCES OR SKILLS YOU HAVE

Write down 3 strengths, skills, or resources you could use to cope if the worst happens:

1. ....

2. ....

3. ....

2: IDENTIFY 2 POSITIVE OUTCOMES THAT COULD OCCUR

List 2 good things that could come from facing this challenge:

1. ....

2. ....

1: IDENTIFY 1 SMALL STEP YOU CAN TAKE RIGHT NOW

Write down 1 small, specific action you can take right now to move forward:

....

....

COMMITMENT TO ACTION

I commit to taking this next step on: ....

How I will reward myself after taking this step:

....

....

....

....

....

....

....

....

....

....

ENDING WEEK 7: REFLECTION AND SUMMARY

Three things I've learned about courage and anxiety:

1. ....

....

2. ....

....

3. ....

....

Small brave steps I've taken this week:

....

....

....

....

....

....

....

....

What I've realized about the relationship between courage and anxiety:

....

....

....

....

....

....

....

A small intention I'm carrying into next week:

....

....

....

....

....

....

REMEMBER: *Courage isn't about not feeling anxious; it's about moving forward even while anxiety is present. Each small step you take builds confidence and expands your world, allowing you to live a rich and meaningful life despite the presence of anxiety. Be proud of each courageous action, no matter how small, because this is how we develop true strength.*

LOVING YOUR ANXIOUS HEART

THE NURTURING HAND

In the journey of dealing with anxiety, we often struggle to find strength, control, or solutions. But sometimes, what we truly need isn't more effort, but deeper compassion - a gentle, tender approach to our experience.

Self-compassion isn't self-pity, but acknowledging that we, like all people, deserve kindness, especially when going through difficult moments. When facing anxiety, the ability to respond to ourselves with gentleness can be a powerful source of strength and healing.

UNDERSTANDING SELF-COMPASSION:

1. Self-kindness instead of self-judgment: Treating yourself with gentleness, understanding, and forgiveness, just as you would treat a good friend.

2. Recognition of common humanity instead of isolation: Recognizing that suffering and failure are part of the shared human experience, not something that makes you alone or abnormal.

3. Mindfulness instead of over-identification with emotions: Maintaining a balanced awareness of thoughts and feelings, neither avoiding nor exaggerating them.

PRACTICING SELF-KINDNESS:

Ask yourself: If a close friend was experiencing anxiety similar to yours, what would you say to them? What tone would you use? How would you express support?

Write a short message you might say to a friend who is anxious:

....

....

....

....

....

Now, write that same message to yourself, as if you were speaking to yourself:

....

....

....

....

....

Is there a difference in how you speak to a friend and how you speak to yourself?

....

....

....

....

SELF-HUG PRACTICE:

A simple but powerful physical act of self-compassion is giving yourself a hug or placing your hand on your heart when feeling anxious. When difficult emotions arise, try these steps:

1. Place one or both hands over your heart, feeling the warmth and gentle pressure.

2. Feel your heartbeat beneath your palm.

3. Breathe gently, imagining the breath moving in and out through the heart area.

4. Say to yourself gently: "This is a difficult moment. I am here with you. I care about this pain."

5. Allow yourself to feel whatever is happening, held in the gentle embrace of your own arms.

Write about your experience with this exercise:

....

....

....

....

THE FRIEND IN THE MIRROR

In moments of anxiety, we often become our own harshest critics. Our inner language can be filled with self-judgment, criticism, and even contempt - words we would never say to a loved one.

Mirror work - the practice of looking into your own eyes in a mirror and speaking words of love - can be a powerful way to break the cycle of self-criticism and nurture a healthier relationship with yourself.

MIRROR WORK PRACTICE:

1. Find a private place with a mirror.

2. Look deeply into your own eyes.

3. Notice your initial reaction - it might be discomfort, embarrassment, or avoidance. Stay with these feelings without judgment.

4. Say one of the phrases below (or one of your own) to yourself, focusing on keeping your tone gentle and sincere:

- "I see you and your pain."
- "You're doing the best you can."
- "I accept you completely as you are."
- "I love you and will always be here for you."

5. Notice the feelings that arise - accept any discomfort or doubt that may emerge.

RECORD YOUR EXPERIENCE:

What initial emotions arose when you looked into your eyes in the mirror?

....

....

....

How did it feel to speak words of love to yourself?

....

....

....

Were there any specific affirmations that felt particularly powerful for you?

....

....

....

....

....

CREATE YOUR OWN AFFIRMATIONS:

Write three loving affirmations that you could say to yourself while looking in the mirror. They should address aspects of yourself that you tend to criticize when anxiety appears:

1. ....

2. ....

3. ....

LULLABIES FOR THE ANXIOUS HEART

When anxiety overwhelms, we often unintentionally amplify our suffering through self-criticism, worrying about the anxiety, and feelings of shame. In such moments, a short self-soothing mantra - like a gentle lullaby - can help break the spiral of self-criticism and bring comfort.

Science has shown that self-soothing words, especially when spoken in a gentle voice, can activate the body's relaxation system, lower cortisol (stress hormone) levels, and create a sense of safety.

CREATE YOUR OWN LULLABY:

An effective lullaby is usually short, gentle, and easy to remember. It can remind you of core truths that are easy to forget when anxiety is high:

Examples:

- "This moment will pass, and I will be okay."

- "I am here with you, breathing together."

- "I hold my heart with tenderness."

- "I am safe enough to feel this."

- "This is just an emotion, and I am larger than it."

Write 2-3 of your own lullabies. Write them here so you can return to them when needed:

....

....

....

....

....

....

PRACTICE WITH YOUR LULLABY:

Choose one of the lullabies you wrote above. Close your eyes, place your hand on your heart, and repeat that lullaby to yourself 10 times, with a gentle voice (can be whispered or in your mind).

After practicing, write about your experience:

....

....

....

....

....

CREATE A CONNECTION BETWEEN YOUR LULLABY AND YOUR BODY:

To make your lullaby more powerful, pair it with a simple physical gesture - like placing your hand on your heart, gently hugging yourself, or touching your thumb to your middle finger. As you practice this gesture with your lullaby multiple times, your brain will begin to associate that gesture with the calm state. Eventually, even if you only perform the gesture without saying the lullaby, your body may still feel the soothing effect.

Describe the gesture you want to pair with your lullaby:

....

....

....

....

....

....

....

....

....

....

....

....

....

....

....

DAILY REFLECTION 1: BEING KIND TO YOURSELF

A LOVING MESSAGE:

Dear friend, remember that anxiety doesn't reflect your worth. It's just a wave of emotion passing through; it doesn't define who you are. Treat yourself as if you were holding a frightened child - with patience, gentleness, and the understanding that these difficult feelings will gradually dissolve. Your pain deserves to be seen and loved. Cherish yourself today, not because you have to do everything perfectly, but simply because you deserve love - today and every day.

Gentle prompt: If I spoke to myself as I would to someone I love...

....

....

....

....

....

....

....

....

....

....

....

....

Reflection question: One way I embraced my pain today...

....

....

....

....

....

....

....

....

....

Loving reminder: The kindest thing I could say to myself when anxiety appears is...

....

....

....

....

....

....

....

....

....

....

DAILY REFLECTION 2: EMBRACING THE WOUNDED PARTS

A LOVING MESSAGE:

The most anxious parts of you are not the enemy. They are parts of you that have endured pain and are now trying to protect you in the only way they know how. Imagine these fearful parts as small children within you, not needing to be judged or fixed, but simply to be embraced and understood. Invite them into the space of your heart. Listen to their fears and worries. Let them know that you are here, that you are strong enough to hold them, and that they no longer have to face the world alone.

Gentle prompt: If I spoke to myself as I would to someone I love...

....

....

....

....

....

....

....

....

....

....

....

Reflection question: One way I embraced my pain today...

....

....

....

....

....

....

....

....

....

Dialogue with your inner child: If you could speak to the small, frightened part of yourself, what would you say?

....

....

....

....

....

....

....

....

....

....

DAILY REFLECTION 3: TRANSFORMING SELF-CRITICISM INTO SELF-COMPASSION

A LOVING MESSAGE:

The self-critical voice often appears strongest when we need gentleness the most. Behind harsh criticism is often fear - fear of not being good enough, fear of failure, fear of being unworthy. Remember that you don't need to be perfect to deserve kindness. In fact, it's in the moments when we feel most flawed that we need compassion the most. When you catch yourself being self-critical, pause, take a deep breath, and ask yourself: "What do I need most right now? How can I meet that need with kindness?"

Gentle prompt: If I spoke to myself as I would to someone I love...

....

....

....

....

....

....

....

....

....

....

....

Reflection question: One way I embraced my pain today...

....

....

....

....

....

....

....

....

Transforming self-criticism:

A recent self-critical thought:

....

....

....

....

How to rewrite it with compassion:

....

....

....

....

....

DAILY REFLECTION 4: NURTURING YOURSELF IN DIFFICULTY

A LOVING MESSAGE:

In your darkest moments, remind yourself that you are going through something, not failing at something. Anxiety is not a sign of weakness or inadequacy - it's simply a human experience that many share. Just as dark clouds don't define the entire sky, anxiety doesn't define your entire being. Beneath these intense emotions exists a space of peace - your core self remains intact, undamaged by any storm. Care for yourself with patience and deep compassion, knowing that you deserve this love simply because you exist.

Gentle prompt: If I spoke to myself as I would to someone I love...

....

....

....

....

....

....

....

....

....

....

....

Reflection question: One way I embraced my pain today...

....

....

....

....

....

....

....

....

....

Self-care action: One kind thing I could do for myself when feeling anxious is...

....

....

....

....

....

....

....

....

....

....

PRACTICING SELF-KINDNESS IN DAILY LIFE:

Self-compassion isn't limited to formal exercises; it can be integrated into your daily life. Here are some simple ways to nurture a more loving relationship with yourself:

1. Transform inner language:

Notice when you speak to yourself with harsh language. Practice "catching" these statements and transforming them into kinder messages. For example:

- Instead of "I'm so useless when I'm this anxious," try "I'm going through a difficult time right now, and that's normal. I'll get through this."

- Instead of "I should be handling this better," try "I'm doing the best I can with the tools I have right now."

2. Daily check-in moment:

Take a moment each day to ask:

- "What do I need most right now?"

- "How can I treat myself most kindly in this moment?"

Then take a small action to meet that need, even if it's just drinking a warm cup of tea in silence, taking 5 minutes to breathe deeply, or calling a friend to connect.

3. The gentle hand:

Practice placing your hand on your heart during daily activities - while sitting in your car, waiting in line, or before sleep. This simple gesture is a physical reminder to treat yourself with gentleness.

4. Dear self letter:

Write a short letter to yourself from the perspective of an unconditionally loving friend. Carry this letter with you and read it when feeling anxious or self-critical.

5. "And" instead of "But":

When you catch yourself being self-critical, instead of saying "I'm anxious, but I should be calmer," try "I'm anxious, and that's okay. I'm doing the best I can."

CREATE YOUR DAILY SELF-COMPASSION PLAN:

Choose 2-3 practices from the list above (or create your own) that you will integrate into your daily life. Write them here:1. Transform inner language:

....

....

....

....

....

....

....

....

....

....

....

....

....

....

....

....

....

ENDING WEEK 8: REFLECTION AND SUMMARY

Three things I've learned about self-compassion:

1. ....

....

2. ....

....

3. ....

....

Changes I've noticed when practicing self-compassion:

....

....

....

....

....

....

....

....

My biggest challenge in maintaining self-compassion is:

....

....

....

....

....

....

....

....

A small intention I'm carrying into next week:

....

....

....

....

....

....

REMEMBER: *Self-compassion is not a luxury or a weakness - it's a necessary foundation for psychological health and resilience. When you learn to respond to your pain with kindness rather than criticism, you not only soothe anxiety but also build inner strength to cope with any challenge life brings. Treat yourself as you would a precious friend - because that's exactly what you are.*

CONNECTING WITH JOY

WHEN JOY VISITS

When we struggle with anxiety, joy can sometimes feel distant or elusive. The anxious mind tends to focus on threats, dangers, and potential problems, often overlooking small moments of joy, satisfaction, or peace that might appear throughout the day.

However, the ability to recognize and connect with joy - even in small, fleeting moments - is an important skill that can expand our experience, nurture resilience, and gradually change our relationship with anxiety.

UNDERSTANDING JOY AMID ANXIETY:

The truth is that joy and anxiety can coexist. You don't need to completely "fix" anxiety before experiencing moments of joy. In fact, nurturing positive experiences can gradually expand your capacity to hold both emotions simultaneously, creating more space for all your emotional experiences.

This isn't about insisting on "positive thinking" or denying difficult feelings. Rather, it's about expanding your experience to include the full spectrum of human emotions, including genuine joy.

EXERCISE: SMALL JOY HUNT:

For the next 24 hours, notice the small joys that appear in your daily life. This isn't about looking for huge, transformative joys, but for small moments that could easily be overlooked:

- The aroma of morning coffee
- The feeling of warm sunlight on your skin
- A child's laughter
- A favorite song unexpectedly playing
- The warmth of a soft blanket
- A kind message from a friend
- The taste of a favorite food
- A moment of natural beauty

List 5-10 small joys you've experienced in the past 24 hours:

1. ....

2. ....

3. ....

4. ....

5. ....

6. ....

7. ....

8. ....

9. ....

10. ....

RECORD YOUR EXPERIENCE:

What happened when you paid attention to small joys? Did you notice more than you expected?

....

....

....

....

....

Did you find it difficult to acknowledge joyful moments while still feeling anxious? If so, what came up?

....

....

....

....

....

SEEDS OF GRATITUDE

Gratitude is one of the most powerful tools we have to shift the mind away from anxiety spirals and connect with positive elements present in our lives. Research shows that regular gratitude practice not only improves mood but can also reduce anxiety symptoms, improve sleep, and even boost immune function.

Gratitude isn't about ignoring difficulties or challenges in your life. Instead, it's widening the lens to include the positive things that coexist with the challenges.

EXERCISE: GRATITUDE GARDEN

Imagine gratitude as seeds that you're planting and nurturing. With each thing you notice and feel grateful for, you're watering these seeds, helping them grow into a rich garden in your heart.

Planting seeds: Write 5 things you feel grateful for right now. They can be simple, everyday things, or deeper ones:

1. ....

2. ....

3. ....

4. ....

5. ....

Nurturing the seed: Choose one of the things you've written and explore it deeper. Why are you grateful for this? How does it contribute to your life? How do you feel when you think about it?

....

....

....

....

....

From gratitude to joy: Gratitude often opens the door to feelings of joy. As you reflect on things you're grateful for, do you notice a gentle feeling of joy arising? Describe this feeling:

....

....

....

....

....

Daily gratitude practice: Commit to a simple daily gratitude practice for the coming week. It might be listing three things you're grateful for each morning, or taking a moment before sleep to reflect on the gifts of the day. Describe the daily gratitude practice you'll try:

....

....

....

....

....

THE FLAVOR OF THE MOMENT

Many of us live life on "autopilot" - eating without really tasting, looking without really seeing, hearing without really listening. Anxiety can exacerbate this tendency, pulling us into our minds rather than allowing us to fully experience what's happening in the present moment.

Practicing sensory mindfulness - paying attention to what we see, hear, taste, smell, and feel - can bring us back to the present moment, where joy is often found.

EXERCISE: MINDFUL EATING

Choose a simple food or drink - an apple, a piece of chocolate, a cup of tea, or anything you enjoy. For this practice to work best, choose something you like but often eat mindlessly.

1. Look: Observe this food carefully. Notice its colors, shape, light and shadows. Pretend you've never seen this item before.

2. Smell: Bring the food close to your nose. Inhale its aroma slowly and intentionally. Is the smell complex or simple? Subtle or strong? Does it evoke any memories or associations?

3. Touch: Feel the food in your hand. Is it heavy or light? What's its temperature? Is its surface smooth, rough, or textured differently?

4. Taste: Place the food in your mouth, but don't bite yet. Feel it on your tongue. Then, slowly bite and chew, noticing the flavors, textures, and sensations. Notice when the flavor changes and saliva is released.

5. Hear: Are there any sounds as you chew? What sounds does this food make?

Record your mindful eating experience:

....

....

....

Expanding sensory mindfulness practice:

Choose another everyday activity and experience it with complete sensory attention - it could be showering, walking, embracing a loved one, or listening to a favorite song. Describe how you might bring full presence to that activity:

....

....

....

....

....

....

....

....

The connection between mindfulness and joy:

Have you noticed a connection between being fully present in the moment and feelings of joy or satisfaction? Describe what you've observed:

....

....

....

....

....

....

....

DAILY REFLECTION 1: SIMPLE JOYS

SIMPLE JOY PROMPT:

Think about today. Whether it was a "good" day or a "difficult" one, there were surely small moments of joy if we pay enough attention to notice them. It might have been morning sunlight through a window, the smell of breakfast, a loved one's laughter, the warmth of a cup of tea, or a favorite song unexpectedly playing.

Gentle prompt: **One small thing that brought me joy today...**

....

....

....

....

....

....

....

....

....

....

....

....

....

I feel grateful for...

....

....

....

....

....

....

....

....

Small thing I'm looking forward to tomorrow:

....

....

....

....

....

....

....

....

....

....

DAILY REFLECTION 2:
JOY IN THE BODY

SIMPLE JOY PROMPT:

Sometimes, joy is distinctly physical - a warm sensation spreading across the chest, a light vibration in the belly, a feeling of lightness or energy, or a natural smile appearing on the lips. As we learn to pay attention to these joyful sensations in the body, they become more recognizable and we can nurture them.

Gentle prompt: One small thing that brought me joy today...

....

....

....

....

....

....

....

....

....

....

....

....

I feel grateful for...

....

....

....

....

....

....

....

Where I feel joy in my body:

....

....

....

....

....

....

....

....

....

....

....

DAILY REFLECTION 3: JOY IN CONNECTION

SIMPLE JOY PROMPT:

Human beings are wired for connection. Even the smallest interactions can bring joy and meaning - a smile with a shopkeeper, a brief conversation with a neighbor, a message from a friend, or deep time with a loved one. These moments of connection, whether big or small, are important sources of nourishment for the spirit.

Gentle prompt: One small thing that brought me joy today...

....

....

....

....

....

....

....

....

....

....

....

....

....

I feel grateful for...

A meaningful moment of connection:

DAILY REFLECTION 4:
JOY IN CREATIVITY

SIMPLE JOY PROMPT:

Creativity exists in all of us, and expressing it can bring profound joy. This doesn't necessarily have to be "big" art - it might be how you arrange your living space, a meal you prepare, a way you solve a problem, a story you tell, or any way you bring creative energy into the world. When we create, we connect with the inherent joy of making something new.

Gentle prompt: One small thing that brought me joy today...

....

....

....

....

....

....

....

....

....

....

....

....

I feel grateful for...

....

....

....

....

....

....

....

....

One way I expressed creativity:

....

....

....

....

....

....

....

....

....

....

Seeking joy when anxious can feel forced or even impossible. But the reality is that small moments of joy and satisfaction can exist alongside even the most difficult emotions.

Here are some ways to nurture joy even in times of anxiety:

1. Lower your goals:

When anxiety is high, don't look for huge, transformative joy. Instead, look for "micro-joys" - tiny moments of positive feeling:

- The warmth of sunlight on your skin for 10 seconds
- The taste of a sip of cool water
- One really deep and satisfying breath
- A small relaxation in any part of your body

2. Practice "Both..." and "And...":

Instead of experiencing emotions in a binary way (either joyful OR anxious), practice a "both/and" approach:

- "I'm feeling anxious AND I can enjoy the taste of this dinner."
- "BOTH anxiety is present AND the sun is shining."
- "I'm going through a difficult time AND I can still feel grateful for this."

3. Collect joyful moments:

Imagine that you're collecting small, colorful pebbles of joy throughout your day. Each time you notice a small moment of positive feeling, imagine that you place it in your pocket and carry it with you.

At the end of the day, take out and look at your "collection." Be surprised by how many moments you might have collected, even on a difficult day.

4. Practice joy-increasing actions:

Psychologists have identified certain activities that tend to increase positive feelings, even when anxiety is present:

- **Physical movement:** Even gentle movement can release endorphins and improve mood

- **Social connection:** Interacting with others, whether in person or online

- **Time in nature:** Even a short period in green space can elevate mood

- **Meditation:** Regular simple mindfulness practices

- **Acts of kindness:** Doing something nice for others

- **Play:** Engaging in activities for pure enjoyment

- **Immersion in art:** Music, film, books, or other art forms

CREATE YOUR "MICRO-JOY" PLAN:

List 5-10 small, accessible activities that typically bring you moments of small joy, even when anxiety is present:

1. ....

2. ....

3. ....

4. ....

5. ....

6. ....

7. ....

8. ....

9. ....

10. ....

ENDING WEEK 9: REFLECTION AND SUMMARY

Three things I've learned about connecting with joy amid anxiety:

1. ....

....

2. ....

....

3. ....

....

The biggest challenges in seeking joy amid anxiety:

....

....

....

....

....

....

....

....

Most effective strategies for nurturing joy for me:

....

....

....

....

....

....

....

A small intention I'm carrying into next week:

....

....

....

....

....

....

REMEMBER: *Nurturing joy while anxious isn't about denying or avoiding difficult feelings. It's about expanding your experience to include the full spectrum of human emotions. As you practice recognizing and connecting with small moments of joy and gratitude, you build deep resilience that will support you through even the most difficult times.*

WEEK 10
INNER STRENGTH

GOLD IN THE CRACKS

In Japan, there is an ancient art called Kintsugi - the art of repairing broken pottery by joining the pieces with gold. Rather than hiding the cracks, this art celebrates them, transforming breaks into a beautiful part of the object's history.

Kintsugi offers a powerful metaphor for our journey with anxiety. Our cracks - the moments of anxiety, fear, and struggle - are not signs of brokenness. They are part of our story. And sometimes, it's through these very cracks that the light of wisdom, strength, and compassion can shine most clearly.

RECOGNIZING STRENGTH IN STRUGGLE:

Everyone faces challenges, but not everyone recognizes the gifts that can be found in moments of struggle. Our challenges, including anxiety, often force us to develop strengths, skills, and qualities that we might never have known if life were always easy.

REFLECTING ON KINTSUGI:

Think about the "cracked" times in your life - moments of deep anxiety or significant challenge. With your more understanding perspective now, what "gold" can you recognize that emerged from those experiences?

Challenging time:...

....

"Gold" I found from this experience: ....
....
....
....

Challenging time: ....
....
....

"Gold" I found from this experience: ....
....
....
....

YOUR OWN KINTSUGI METAPHOR:

Imagine yourself as a Kintsugi work in progress, healing and becoming stronger. Golden lines are connecting and highlighting the beauty of your whole self. Draw or describe yourself as a Kintsugi work - marking where the gold lines are (the strengths you've found through challenges)

[Space for drawing/writing]

MY STORY, MY STRENGTH

The way we tell the story of our lives has tremendous power. Research on "narrative coherence" shows that people who can create meaning from their experiences and see themselves as protagonists rather than victims in their own stories tend to demonstrate greater resilience and can cope better with anxiety.

Rather than viewing anxiety as a flaw or enemy, we can begin to tell a new story: one in which anxiety has played a role in leading us to inner strengths and wisdom we might not have discovered otherwise.

REWRITING YOUR ANXIETY STORY:

Describe your experience with anxiety as if you were telling a meaningful story. You are the protagonist - not a passive victim, but a brave person facing a challenge.

In the beginning...

....
....
....
....

Then...

....
....
....

And now...

....
....
....

IDENTIFYING STORY THEMES:

Read back through the story you just wrote. What themes do you notice about strength, growth, or wisdom?

....

....

....

NEW TITLE FOR YOUR STORY:

If your story with anxiety were a book, what would the title be? Choose a title that reflects strength and growth, not just struggle.

....

....

....

ROOTS AND WINGS:

A strong tree needs both a sturdy root system diving deep into the ground, and branches reaching high toward the light. Similarly, to truly grow through anxiety, we need both to be firmly rooted - connected to our core values and strengths; and to spread our wings - expanding and growing beyond what we once thought possible.

ROOTING: CONNECTING TO CORE VALUES AND STRENGTHS

When facing anxiety, staying connected to what matters most to us is essential. Our core values such as love, compassion, integrity, or creativity can be sources of strength even in very difficult moments.

List 5 values most important to you:

1. ....

2. ....

3. ....

4. ....

5. ....

Choose one of these values and describe how it can support you in moments of anxiety:

....

....

....

....

....

....

SPREADING WINGS: GROWTH AND EXPANSION

Anxiety often makes us contract and shrink. To counter this tendency, we can intentionally "spread our wings" - challenging ourselves to grow, learn, and expand beyond self-imposed limitations.

List 3 ways you might "spread your wings" in the coming weeks - small things that might push you slightly beyond your comfort zone:

1. ....

....

2. ....

....

3. ....

....

THE BALANCE OF ROOTING AND WINGING:

What helps you feel rooted and connected to your true self?

....

....

....

....

....

What helps you feel like you're growing and reaching higher?

....

....

....

....

....

VISUALIZATION: TREE OF INNER STRENGTH

Take a moment to imagine yourself as a strong tree, with deep roots and branches reaching high:

1. Imagine your roots growing deep into the earth, connecting with core values, relationships, and beliefs.

2. Feel your sturdy trunk, representing your stable presence in the world.

3. Visualize your branches extending in all directions, with new leaves and buds - representing your growth, learning, and potential.

4. Notice the tree's ability to bend but not break in the wind - representing your flexibility and resilience.

Describe your "tree of inner strength":

DAILY REFLECTION 1: STRENGTH FROM DIFFICULTY

A STORY ABOUT OVERCOMING DIFFICULTY:

After a serious car accident, Elena had to endure months of physical and psychological recovery. She developed a fear of driving and anxiety when traveling on roads. Rather than viewing the accident as purely a tragedy, Elena gradually began to recognize unexpected gifts from the experience: a deeper capacity for empathy with others' pain, a greater appreciation for simple walks, and a clearer sense of what truly matters in life. "I would never wish for that accident to happen," she says, "but I also no longer look at it as just a disaster. It's part of my story that makes me who I am today, and there are parts of who I am now that I'm genuinely grateful for."

Gentle prompt: A strength I found within myself today...

....

....

....

....

....

....

....

....

....

....

....

Reflection question: A difficulty that has taught me...

....

....

....

....

....

....

....

....

....

Another way of seeing: A difficult experience that I can now look at with gratitude is...

....

....

....

....

....

....

....

....

....

....

DAILY REFLECTION 2: THE POWER OF CHOICE

A STORY ABOUT OVERCOMING DIFFICULTY:

Marcus had battled social anxiety for many years. He found himself increasingly avoiding social situations and feeling as though anxiety was controlling his life. In a breakthrough moment, he realized that while he couldn't always control when anxious feelings arose, he could choose his response to them. "I truly realized that even when I feel completely anxious, I can still choose to move forward with things that matter to me," he shares. "Just recognizing this helped me feel less powerless. I still feel anxious at social events, but now I know that my presence there is a choice I'm making, a brave act based on my values. It completely changed the meaning of social gatherings for me."

Gentle prompt: A strength I found within myself today...

....

....

....

....

....

....

....

....

....

....

....

Reflection question: A difficulty that has taught me...

....

....

....

....

....

....

....

....

....

The power of choice: A small choice I can make today despite anxiety is...

....

....

....

....

....

....

....

....

....

....

....

DAILY REFLECTION 3: THE POWER OF NEW RULES

A STORY ABOUT OVERCOMING DIFFICULTY:

As a child, Sophia was taught to "always be strong," which meant never showing worry or insecurity. As an adult, she developed chronic anxiety and deep shame about her "weakness." Through years of working with herself, Sophia gradually rewrote these rules. "I created a new set of rules for myself," she explains. "The first rule is 'Allow all emotions to be present.' The second rule is 'True strength includes vulnerability.' And the most important rule is 'I don't need to be anyone but my authentic self.'" These new rules became a source of strength and guidance, allowing her to be whole with herself, including her anxious parts, rather than constantly trying to hide them away.

Gentle prompt: A strength I found within myself today...

....

....

....

....

....

....

....

....

....

....

....

Reflection question: A difficulty that has taught me...

....

....

....

....

....

....

....

....

....

....

....

....

New rule: An old rule I used to follow was...

....

....

....

The new rule I'm creating for myself is..

....

....

DAILY REFLECTION 4: THE POWER OF CONNECTION

A STORY ABOUT OVERCOMING DIFFICULTY:

After years of struggling with anxiety alone, David finally reached out to a support group. "I always believed I needed to figure everything out by myself," he shares. "Admitting my anxiety to others seemed like admitting some kind of failure." But as he listened to others tell their stories, something remarkable happened. "I realized that I wasn't alone, and moreover, that real strength wasn't about not needing anyone, but having the courage to connect and share with others." Through this experience, he discovered that opening up to others not only reduced feelings of isolation but was a tremendous source of strength. "There's an amazing power in being seen and accepted by others, exactly as you are, with all your struggles."

Gentle prompt: A strength I found within myself today...

....

....

....

....

....

....

....

....

....

....

Reflection question: A difficulty that has taught me...

....

....

....

....

....

Strength from connection: A relationship that gives me strength when I'm anxious is...

....

....

....

....

....

SOURCES OF STRENGTH IN ANXIETY

Paradoxically, anxiety - which can feel like a sign of weakness - can actually become a source of great strength when we learn to approach it with a growth mindset.

Here are some powerful qualities that can develop when working with your anxiety:

1. Stronger self-awareness

Anxiety, when approached with curiosity, can help you develop a deeper understanding of yourself - your core beliefs, values, and needs. People who work with their anxiety often develop superior emotional intelligence - the ability to recognize and understand their own and others' emotions.

Ways anxiety has helped you understand yourself better:

....

....

....

2. Deeper compassion

Experiencing anxiety can teach us profound compassion - both for ourselves and others. When we know how deep mental pain can be, we develop a powerful capacity for empathy and a deep understanding of others' struggles.

Ways anxiety has deepened your compassion:

....

....

....

....

3. Proven resilience

Each time you experience a moment of anxiety and move through it, you're building evidence of your resilience - proof that you can face uncomfortable feelings and still continue.

A moment when you demonstrated resilience in the face of anxiety:

....

....

....

....

4. True courage

Courage isn't about not feeling fear - it's about acting despite fear. People living with anxiety regularly demonstrate this type of courage, even when others can't see it.

A way in which dealing with anxiety has required courage:

....

....

....

5. Capacity to accept uncertainty

Anxiety often revolves around unknowns, and learning to live with anxiety often means developing a deeper capacity to accept uncertainty - an invaluable skill in life

Ways anxiety has taught you about living with uncertainty:

....

....

....

OTHER PERSONAL QUALITIES:

Beyond those listed above, what other qualities or personal strengths can you recognize that have developed through your experience with anxiety?

....

....

....

ENDING WEEK 10: REFLECTION AND SUMMARY

Three things I've discovered about my inner strength:

1. ....

....

2. ....

....

3. ....

....

How my view of anxiety has changed over the past 10 weeks:

....

....

....

....

....

....

....

....

An inner strength I want to nurture more is:

....

....

....

....

....

....

....

A small intention I'm carrying into next week:

....

....

....

....

....

....

REMEMBER: *We often find our greatest strengths not when things become easy, but when we face challenges and discover our capacity to overcome. Anxiety may feel like an obstacle, but it can also be a doorway to sources of strength and wisdom you never knew you had. As you continue this journey, increasingly recognize the qualities, skills, and inner resources that have been within you all along.*

BUILDING A LOVING LIFE

THE HOME OF THE HEART

Our daily lives are made up of small habits, relationships, spaces, and activities. When anxiety becomes part of life, proactively building a lifestyle that nurtures peace and safety becomes extremely important.

Creating a "home" for your heart isn't just about avoiding anxiety-provoking situations. It's about actively building a life where you can feel supported, nourished, and safe enough to face challenges when they arise.

ELEMENTS OF A LOVING LIFE:

A loving life typically includes a balance of the following elements:

1. **Meaningful connections** - Relationships where you feel understood, accepted, and supported

2. **Rhythms and rituals** - Reliable patterns that create a sense of stability

3. **Regular self-care** - Practices that nourish both body and mind

4. **Healthy boundaries** - Clear limits that protect your energy and space

5. **Safe spaces** - Physical environments that foster peace

6. **Purpose and meaning** - Activities that reflect your values and vision

7. **Self-expression** - Ways to express your emotions and thoughts

DESIGNING YOUR LIFE:

Imagine that you're intentionally creating your life, like an architect designs a house. You're building this space to nurture the best, healthiest version of yourself.

Using the space below, draw a diagram of your "ideal life home." You can draw an actual house with different rooms representing aspects of life, or use a chart, list, or any creative form:

[Space for drawing/writing]

IDENTIFYING GAPS:

Compare your "ideal home" with your current life:

- Which elements of your vision are already present in your current life?
- What are the biggest gaps between your current life and your ideal life?
- What small changes might help you move closer to your vision?

Record your observations:

LOVING BOUNDARIES

Boundaries are invisible limits that define what we allow in our lives and relationships. When anxiety is part of life, boundaries become especially important - not as barriers to separate us from the world, but as supportive frameworks that help us engage with life in a healthy way.

UNDERSTANDING BOUNDARIES:

Contrary to common thinking, strong boundaries actually allow us to connect more deeply with others. When we know we're protected, we can open up more easily. Healthy boundaries aren't walls, but gates - allowing us to choose when to open and when to close.

People living with anxiety often struggle with boundaries in different ways:

- **Too thin boundaries:** Feeling unable to say "no," taking excessive responsibility for others' emotions, easily overwhelmed by others' needs
- **Too rigid boundaries:** Difficulty opening up, blocking intimacy, isolating to avoid hurt
- **Inconsistent boundaries:** Swinging between extremes, creating unpredictable relationships

CREATING LOVING BOUNDARIES:

Healthy boundaries come from self-respect, not fear. They come from recognizing your worth and caring enough to protect your energy and space. Here's how to practice:

1. Listen to your body: The body often knows before the mind when boundaries are being crossed. Notice feelings of restlessness, tension, or discomfort.

2. Recognize what works for you: Think of a specific situation. Complete these sentences:

- I feel comfortable when: ....
- I feel uncomfortable when: ....
- I need: ....

3. Practice boundary communication:

- "I can help you tomorrow. Today, I need time for myself."
- "I'm not comfortable with this topic. Can we talk about something else?"
- "I care about you, but I can't solve this problem for you."

• "Thank you for the invitation, but my answer is no."

4. Practice self-reflection: After setting a boundary, notice feelings like guilt or anxiety. Remember that these feelings often come from old beliefs and don't reflect the reality of setting healthy boundaries.

VISUALIZING HEALTHY BOUNDARIES:

Imagine your boundaries as a beautiful fence surrounding a sacred garden. This fence has gates that you can intentionally open when you choose to welcome others.

Draw or describe your boundary "fence." What does it look like, what is it made of? Where are the gates located and what do they look like?

[Space for drawing/writing]

THE RHYTHM OF CARE

Self-care is not a single activity but a way of living - a rhythm of activities, habits, and practices woven into the fabric of your day, week, and seasons. When anxiety is part of life, these rhythms become crucially important anchors, creating a sense of stability and reassurance.

DAILY RHYTHMS:

A nurturing daily rhythm creates anchor points throughout the day — moments that your nervous system can rely on. These simple activities can become "home" when anxiety appears.

Design an ideal daily rhythm, including at least one self-care practice for:

• **Morning** (e.g., 5 minutes of writing, quiet tea, gentle stretching)

....

....

....

• **Mid-day** (e.g., in-place walking, device-free lunch, 2-minute deep breathing)

....

....

....

• **Evening** (e.g., tea ritual, gratitude journaling, reading)

....

....

....

• **Before sleep** (e.g., body relaxation, speaking words of gratitude, gentle heart tapping)

....

....

....

....

....

WEEKLY RHYTHMS:

Beyond daily rhythms, weekly self-care practices can provide addition-al structure and support. This is an opportunity to invest more deeply in your physical, mental, and emotional wellbeing.

Design a weekly rhythm, allocating at least one deeper care activity for each of these areas:

• **Physical self-care** (e.g., longer walk, swimming, yoga)

....

....

....

....

• **Emotional self-care** (e.g., journaling, support group, coaching)

....

....

....

....

• **Mental self-care** (e.g., meditation, forest walk, religious practice)

....

....

....

• **Social self-care** (e.g., meeting friends, community activity, calling a relative)

....

....

....

• **Creative self-care** (e.g., drawing, gardening, cooking, music)

....

....

....

....

....

....

....

FROM RITUAL TO SANCTUARY:

As you practice these rhythms and rituals regularly, they become sanctuaries - safe spaces you can return to when anxiety appears. Here are some ways to transform rituals into sanctuaries:

1. Incorporate mindfulness: Perform each ritual with full attention, using all your senses.

2. Add intention: Begin each ritual with a simple affirmation or intention such as "I am nurturing peace within me" or "This is my time."

3. Create sacred space: Designate a specific space for practice, even if just a small corner of a room, and make it special.

4. Embrace symbolism: Incorporate meaningful objects into your ritual, such as a special cup for tea, a scarf for yoga, or a candle for meditation.

5. Accept imperfection: Rhythms don't need to be perfect to be effective. Even if you can only do a shorter or simplified version, consistency matters more than perfection.

Describe a care ritual that you would like to develop into a sanctuary. How will you perform it, and how will it nourish you?

DAILY REFLECTION 1: CREATING A NEST FOR THE HEART

A STORY ABOUT CREATING SAFE SPACE:

Emily realized that her apartment — the place she returned to every day — didn't really feel like a sanctuary. Her living space was cluttered with unfinished projects, scattered items, and rushed energy. Her mornings were hurried and tense, and her evenings were often an extension of work and tasks.

After a particularly intense bout of anxiety, Emily decided to transform her home into a "nest for the heart." She began by clearing one small corner — creating a quiet space with a comfortable chair, a plant, and a soft lamp. Each morning, instead of checking emails immediately, she spent 10 minutes sitting in this corner, enjoying a cup of tea and setting an intention for the day.

Gradually, Emily extended that sense of peace and intention to the entire apartment — decluttering spaces, adding small items that brought joy, and creating simple rituals that marked the beginning and end of each day. The change wasn't just in the physical space, but in the feeling of coming home. The house had become an outer symbol for the inner home she was building — a safe place for her heart to rest.

Gentle prompt: How I made a nest for myself today...

....

....

....

....

....

....

Reflection question: A place or space that gives me a feeling of safety and peace is...

....

....

....

....

....

....

....

....

Elements of nesting: Three elements I could add to my living space to nurture peace are...

....

....

....

....

....

....

....

....

....

DAILY REFLECTION 2:
THE HOUSE OF VALUES

A STORY ABOUT LIVING BY VALUES:

After years of trying to please others and building a life based on others' expectations, Alex felt exhausted and disconnected. Anxiety steadily increased as he realized he was living a life that didn't truly reflect what he cared about most deeply.

In a life design course, Alex was invited to identify his core values. Initially, he struggled to recognize his actual values versus what he thought he should value. Through weeks of questioning, Alex identified his top three values: creativity, connection, and contribution.

Alex began evaluating every aspect of his life against these values. He realized his job had almost no opportunities for creativity, many of his relationships were fairly shallow, and he rarely felt he was making a difference. Step by step, Alex began rebuilding his life:

He joined a weekly art class to nurture his creativity; spent quality time with a few close friends instead of superficial socializing; and volunteered for an organization helping youth. Over time, he even transitioned to a new role that allowed him to use his design skills.

As Alex built his life house on the foundation of personal values, anxiety didn't completely disappear, but it no longer overwhelmed. There was a deep sense of authenticity that came from living true to himself.

Gentle prompt: How I made a nest for myself today...

....

....

....

....

Reflection question: A core value I want my life to reflect more is...

....

....

....

....

....

....

....

....

....

Small action: One small action that could help me live more aligned with this value is...

....

....

....

....

....

....

....

....

....

....

DAILY REFLECTION 3: BOUNDARIES OF THE HEART

A STORY ABOUT SETTING BOUNDARIES:

Lisa had always prided herself on being there for others. An excellent listener and problem-solver, she was often the first person friends and colleagues turned to in difficulty. While she loved this supportive role, signs of burnout began appearing — frequent headaches, insomnia, and increasing anxiety.

In therapy, Lisa realized that her boundaries were almost non-existent. She rarely said "no," was always available for texts or calls, and routinely put others' needs above her own. Her therapist explained that healthy boundaries weren't selfish but necessary — not just for her health but for the quality of presence she could bring to others.

Lisa began practicing small boundaries: putting her phone on silent after 8 PM, waiting at least an hour before responding to non-urgent messages, and dedicating one weekend day to "filling her cup" rather than "pouring out." At first, she felt guilty and worried that others would feel abandoned. But as she continued to practice, she realized that people still respected and valued her, and her relationships actually deepened.

A breakthrough moment came when Lisa realized that by setting boundaries, she was creating an example for others — especially younger women — that self-care isn't selfish but essential. Her boundaries not only protected her inner home but became an act of love andresponsibility to the wider community.

Gentle prompt: How I made a nest for myself today...

....

....

....

....

....

Reflection question: I say "yes" to... and "no" to...

....

....

....

....

....

....

....

....

Boundary practice: A situation where I need to set clearer boundaries is...

....

....

....

....

....

....

....

....

....

....

DAILY REFLECTION 4: SACRED RHYTHMS

A STORY ABOUT DAILY RHYTHMS:

When Marcus was diagnosed with anxiety disorder, he felt overwhelmed by the multitude of suggested tools and techniques. Meditation, journaling, exercise, gratitude practice, breathing... the list seemed endless. Trying to do everything at once only added to feelings of failure and stress.

Marcus's therapist suggested a different approach: "Instead of trying to do everything, choose one small practice for morning, one for midday, and one for evening. Perform these practices regularly not as tasks, but as sacred rituals — holy moments in your day."

Marcus started simply: three minutes of breath meditation in the morning, a short midday walk, and a three-item gratitude list before sleep. What made these practices different was how he approached them — not as items to check off a to-do list, but as important rituals marking the rhythm of the day.

Marcus created small symbols to enhance the sense of sacredness: a special meditation cushion for mornings, a familiar path with a favorite bench for the midday walk, and a beautiful notebook beside the bed for the evening gratitude list. Over time, Marcus noticed that he not only looked forward to these moments, but found they had become anchors for him throughout the day.

"I don't need to do everything," he realized. "I just need to establish rhythm that my soul can rely on."

Gentle prompt: How I made a nest for myself today...

....

....

....

....

Reflection question: A rhythm or ritual I want to build into my daily life is...

....

....

....

....

....

....

....

....

Making it sacred: How could I transform this activity from a task into a sacred ritual?

....

....

....

....

....

....

....

....

....

LAYERED LIFE DESIGN

As we continue building a loving life, arranging activities intentionally into "layers" can help us create a sense of balance and support. This is particularly helpful for managing chronic anxiety.

THE LAYERS OF LIFE:

Imagine that your life consists of different layers of activities, each serving a specific purpose in nurturing your overall wellbeing:

1. Physical self-care - Essential daily practices that create the base (sleep, nutrition, housekeeping, finances)

2. Stability layer - Activities that provide a sense of safety and structure (rituals, routines, clear limits)

3. Connection layer - Activities that nurture meaningful relationships (time with loved ones, calls with friends, community gatherings)

4. Nourishment layer - Activities that restore and nurture you (forest bathing, art, reading, meditation)

5. Growth layer - Activities that promote development and learning (courses, new challenges, personal goals)

6. Transformation layer - Activities that connect you to something larger than yourself (meditation, volunteering, spirituality)

DESIGNING LIFE BY ARRANGING LAYERS:

Assess your current life. How much time and energy are you putting into each layer? Are there any layers being neglected?

For many people living with anxiety, the foundation and stability layers need to be prioritized before focusing heavily on higher layers. As you feel stabilized, you can gradually expand to other layers.

In the space below, design your "life cake," designating specific activities you want to include in each layer:

- **Foundation layer** (Activities necessary to maintain basic stability):

....

....

....

....

....

....

- **Stability layer** (Activities that provide a sense of safety and structure):

....

....

....

....

- **Connection layer** (Activities that nurture relationships):

....

....

....

....

....

- **Nourishment layer** (Activities that restore and nurture):

....

....

....

- **Growth layer** (Activities that promote development and learning):

....

....

....

....

....

....

- **Transformation layer** (Activities that connect you to something larger):

....

....

....

....

....

....

BALANCE AND SEASONALITY:

Not every phase of life requires the same balance. During challenging or transitional times, you may need to focus more on the lower layers. During stable times, you may have space for more growth and transformation activities.

Be compassionate with yourself and adjust your plan as needed. The goal is not perfection, but balance and intention.

For this season in your life, which layer needs the most attention? How can you ensure you're nurturing those layers?

ENDING WEEK 11: REFLECTION AND SUMMARY

Three things I've learned about building a loving life:

1. ....

....

2. ....

....

3. ....

....

A small change I've made in how I design my life:

....

....

....

....

....

....

....

....

The importance of boundaries and rhythms for a balanced life:

....

....

....

....

....

....

....

A small intention I'm carrying into next week:

....

....

....

....

....

....

REMEMBER: *Building a loving life isn't about creating a perfect life without stress or anxiety. It's about creating a structure and space where you can feel supported when facing challenges, have enough room to breathe when emotions rise, and be surrounded by what nourishes your soul. Each small step toward a life that better aligns with your true values and needs is important and worthy of appreciation.*

THE PATH FOR-WARD

REFLECTING ON THE RIVER

We've come a long way together. Over the past 11 weeks, you've met your anxiety, explored the power of breath, listened to the wisdom of your body, and learned to stand strong in the storm. You've practiced listening to inner voices, expanding space for emotions, taking small brave steps, and cultivating self-compassion. You've connected with joy, discovered inner strength, and begun building a loving life.

This journey, as I mentioned at the beginning, isn't a straight line from "anxiety" to "peace." It's a winding river, sometimes flowing smoothly, sometimes creating rapids, sometimes forming still pools, but always moving forward.

This final week isn't a "destination." Instead, it's a moment to look back at your journey, acknowledge your growth, and prepare for the path ahead – the path you'll continue to walk with greater wisdom and compassion.

LOOKING BACK AT THE RIVER:

Take some time now to look back at your 90-day journey. In the space below, draw the "river" of your journey, marking important moments – discoveries, challenges, changes, or breakthrough moments. You can draw an actual river with bends, rapids, and still waters, or use any visual metaphor that resonates with you.

[Space for drawing/writing]

REFLECTING ON THE JOURNEY:

Looking at the "river" you've just drawn, reflect on these questions:

• What was the most challenging thing you experienced in this journey?

• What was the most surprising or unexpected thing you discovered?

• Which practice had the most profound impact on you?

• What changes have you noticed in how you experience and respond to anxiety?

• What are the most valuable lessons you've learned?

TOOLS FOR THE JOURNEY

As you continue on the path forward, returning to daily life without the guidance of this journal, it's important to recognize the tools, skills, and understandings you've developed – the toolkit you'll carry with you on the journey ahead.

PERSONAL TOOLKIT:

Below, create a specific list of your "personal toolkit" – the techniques, practices, and approaches you found most helpful:

When anxiety is mild (First signs, when you're beginning to feel tense):

1. ....

2. ....

3. ....

When anxiety is moderate (Clearly present, affecting your day):

1. ....

2. ....

3. ....

When anxiety is strong (Moments of crisis, feeling overwhelmed):

1. ....

2. ....

3. ....

For building long-term resilience (Preventive/daily practices):

1. ....

2. ....

3. ....

GUIDING QUESTIONS:

Sometimes, powerful questions can guide us toward understanding and clarity. From this journey, which questions have become most valuable to you – questions you can ask yourself in challenging moments?

List 3-5 powerful questions you want to keep with you:

1. ....

2. ....

3. ....

4. ....

5. ....

Through this journey, you may have developed certain principles or mantras — core truths about living healthily with anxiety. These are concise wisdoms you can remember and remind yourself of.

For example: "Emotions don't define me, but they carry messages I can learn from" or "I can feel afraid AND still move forward."

Write down 3-5 guiding principles you've developed:

1. ....

2. ....

3. ....

4. ....

5. ....

LETTER TO THE FUTURE

One of the most powerful ways to mark the end of this journey and the beginning of the next phase is to write a letter to your future self. This letter will serve as a bridge between the "you" of today and the "you" of tomorrow — a place to record your growth, promises to yourself, and wisdom you want to remember.

LETTER TO THE FUTURE:

Write a letter to yourself in the future — perhaps a week, a month, or a year from now. You might include:

• What you've learned and want to remember

• Advice for challenging moments

• Words that helped you

• Techniques that worked

• Promises you want to keep to yourself

• Changes you've noticed

• Hopes for the future

Dear Future ....,

[Space for writing letter]

With love and understanding, ... today

TIME TO OPEN:

Decide when you'll read this letter again. It could be a specific date in the future, or a moment when you feel you need a reminder of your journey.

I will open this letter on: ....

DAILY REFLECTION 1: WISDOM FOUND

Gentle prompt: What I know now that I didn't know before...

....

....

....

....

....

....

Our journeys often take us to places of understanding we couldn't have imagined before. Insights can arrive suddenly like a flash of lightning, or emerge gradually like a sunrise — but they change how we see the world and ourselves.

It's important to acknowledge these "aha" moments — the truths you've discovered on your journey with anxiety. They don't have to be grand or complex truths. Sometimes, the simplest wisdoms are the most transformative.

Reflection question: A transformative truth I've learned about anxiety is...

....

....

....

....

....

....

Source of wisdom: This truth came to me through... (A specific practice? A difficult moment? Quiet reflection?)

....

....

....

....

....

....

....

....

Moving forward: How I will keep this insight in mind as I continue to move forward...

....

....

....

....

....

....

....

....

....

DAILY REFLECTION 2: RITES OF PASSAGE

Gentle prompt: What I know now that I didn't know before…

....

....

....

....

....

....

In many cultures, rites of passage mark the end of one phase and the beginning of another. These rituals aren't merely symbolic — they help our minds, bodies, and spirits adjust and acknowledge the shift that has occurred.

As this 90-day journey concludes, you might find value in creating a small rite of passage — a way to mark, honor, and integrate what you've experienced. This ritual can be simple or complex, but should hold personal meaning for you.

Reflection question: A simple ritual I could create to mark the end of this journey and the beginning of the next phase is…

....

....

....

....

....

....

Ritual elements: To make this ritual meaningful, I will include... (Meaningful objects? Special space? Symbolic actions? Words or intentions?)

....
....
....
....
....
....
....
....
....

Implementation: When and where will I perform this ritual?

....
....
....
....
....
....
....
....
....
....

DAILY REFLECTION 3: HONORING THE JOURNEY

Gentle prompt: What I know now that I didn't know before...

....

....

....

....

....

....

An important part of concluding any journey is pausing to honor what has transpired — not just the destinations you've reached, but also the steps you've taken, the challenges you've faced, and the growth that has occurred along the way.

When we rush from one goal or challenge to another, we can miss this important opportunity to acknowledge growth and integrate lessons learned. Taking time to truly honor your journey is a gift you give yourself.

Reflection question: A few things I'm most proud of about how I approached this journey...

....

....

....

....

....

....

Challenge and growth: A challenge I faced in this journey, and how I grew through it...

....

....

....

....

....

....

....

....

....

Gratitude: I want to express gratitude to myself for...

....

....

....

....

....

....

....

....

....

DAILY REFLECTION 4: THE GIFT OF ANXIETY

Gentle prompt: What I know now that I didn't know before...

....

....

....

....

....

From the beginning of the journey, we've explored the idea that anxiety isn't simply an enemy to be defeated. Instead, like all emotions, it can contain messages and even gifts — if we're willing to listen.

This might be one of the most profound shifts in the journey with anxiety: from seeing it solely as an obstacle or enemy to recognizing that, in some strange way, it can also be a teacher.

This doesn't mean you need to like anxiety or invite it more frequently. Rather, it's an acknowledgment that the experience — though difficult — has brought gifts, lessons, and growth you might not have gained otherwise.

Reflection question: The gift anxiety has given me is...

....

....

....

....

....

Surprising discovery: The most surprising thing about viewing anxiety as a potential teacher is...

....

....

....

....

....

....

....

....

....

Transformative legacy: How my new relationship with anxiety might change my future...

....

....

....

....

....

....

....

....

....

....

AUTUMN TREES AND SPRING SEEDS

As we come to the end of this 90-day journey, a metaphor from nature might help us understand this transition: the image of autumn trees releasing their vibrant leaves, preparing for winter, while the seeds of future spring are already nestled in the soil.

FALLING LEAVES – WHAT YOU CAN RELEASE:

Every transformative journey includes both what we gain AND what we leave behind – old beliefs, habits that no longer serve us, limiting views of ourselves.

In the space below, draw a tree with falling leaves. On each leaf, write something you're ready to release – a limiting belief, an unhealthy habit, an old approach to anxiety, or anything else you feel ready to leave behind.

[Space for drawing/writing]

SEEDS – WHAT YOU'RE NURTURING:

At the same time, your journey has planted new seeds – practices, beliefs, capacities, and understandings that you'll continue to nurture in the seasons ahead.

In the space below, draw seeds nestled in the soil. Beside or inside each seed, write something you're taking from this journey – a new skill, an insight, a different way of seeing yourself, or a practice you'll continue to nurture.

[Space for drawing/writing]

COMMITMENT TO CARE:

Seeds need care to grow. Water, light, time, and patience are all necessary.

Write a brief commitment to yourself about how you'll continue to nurture these seeds in the future:

....

....

....

....

....

....

....

....

....

....

ENDING WEEK 12: REFLECTION AND SUMMARY

Three most important things I take away from this 90-day journey:

1. ....

....

2. ....

....

3. ....

....

How I've changed in my approach to anxiety:

....

....

....

....

....

....

....

Reminders for challenging moments in the future:

....

....

....

....

....

....

....

My commitment to myself as I continue this journey:

....

....

....

....

....

....

REMEMBER: *The end of this 90-day journey isn't the end of growth and healing. It's simply a milestone on a longer path – the path of a whole, authentic life. The insights, tools, and capacities you've developed will continue to serve you, evolve over time, and support you in facing life's challenges. Treat yourself with kindness on both good days and difficult ones, and remember that this is a lifelong journey – not a destination.*

PART III

TOOLKIT FROM THE HEART

Welcome to the final section of this journal – a collection of tools, comforting words, and creative spaces you can return to whenever needed. These aren't mere tools, but gifts from the heart – created with empathy and deep understanding of the journey with anxiety.

In this section, you'll find:

→ Whispers for when the storm comes: Encouraging words and guidance for especially difficult moments

→ Healing passages: Guided meditations and visualizations to bring peace and healing

→ Your creative space: Where you can create your own personal healing tools

Think of this section as a close friend – always ready to accompany you when needed. You can turn here whenever you feel anxious, when you need a loving voice, or when you want to find peace again.

WHISPERS FOR WHEN THE STORM COMES

"EMBRACING PANIC" CARDS

Panic attacks can arrive like a sudden storm - overwhelming, frightening, and sometimes feeling life-threatening. In those moments, simple, gentle words can be a lifeline - reminding us of truths easily forgotten when anxiety takes over.

Below is a collection of comfort cards for panic attacks. You can read them while experiencing a panic attack, or have a loved one read them to you. You might even cut them out and carry them with you as reminders.

CARD 1: THINGS YOU CAN DO RIGHT NOW

Dear Heart,

Try one of these simple things:

- Place your hand on your heart and feel the beating
- Focus on feeling your feet against the floor
- Look around and count five things you can see
- Touch a nearby object and notice its texture
- Close your eyes and listen to the sounds around you
- Suck on a mint or take a sip of water

These small actions can bring you back to the present moment. You don't need to escape the feeling - just add something else alongside it.

CARD 2: RETURN TO BREATH

Dear Heart,

Right now, gently place your attention on your breath. No need to change it - just observe. Feel the air coming in and going out.

Breathe in: I am safe. Breathe out: I let go. Breathe in: This present moment. Breathe out: I allow my body to soften.

Panic is NOT YOU. It's just an experience passing through you. Breath is sanctuary.

CARD 3: YOU ARE NOT ALONE

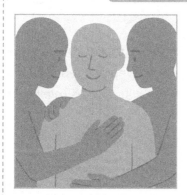

Dear Heart,

Right now, across the world, thousands of people are also experiencing panic attacks - feeling just as you're feeling. You are not broken. You are not weak. You are part of the human family.

I am here with you. We will get through this together. You don't need to be strong, perfect, or "okay." Just be here, breathe, feel.

CARD 4: THIS WILL PASS

Dear Heart,

What you're experiencing is real, but it isn't forever. Panic attacks are like waves - they rise, peak, and recede. No panic attack lasts forever. Your body cannot maintain this state indefinitely.

Remember: you've gotten through this before. And you will get through this time too. You are safe. The storm will pass.

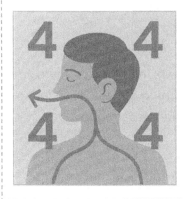

Dear Heart,

Try this 4-4-4-4 technique:

- Breathe in through your nose and count to 4
- Hold your breath and count to 4
- Breathe out through your mouth and count to 4
- Pause before breathing in again, counting to 4

Repeat 4 times, or until you feel calmer. If this formula is difficult, simply focus on lengthening your exhale. Long, slow exhales are the key.

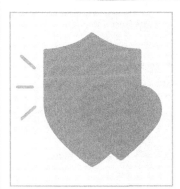

Dear Heart,

The sensations in your body are real, but your mind's interpretation may not be accurate. Racing heart doesn't mean heart attack. Dizziness doesn't mean you'll faint. Shortness of breath doesn't mean you'll stop breathing.

Your body is activating its "fight or flight" system - a protective response. There is no actual danger present. You are safe. Your body is trying to protect you, although unnecessarily.

Dear Heart,

Anxiety pulls us into the future. Gently bring your attention back to this moment. Just this moment. Not five minutes from now. Not tomorrow. Just right now.

In this moment: *You are still breathing. Your heart is still beating. You are still safe. Just be in this moment.*

"WHEN NIGHT FALLS AND ANXIETY WAKES" CARDS

Nighttime anxiety has a character all its own. In darkness, fears seem larger, worries seem more urgent, and everything can feel lonelier. Here are cards to accompany you during those sleepless nights.

CARD 1: SLEEP AND WAVES

Sleepy Heart,

Sleep is like ocean waves - when we try to grasp it, it slips through our fingers. When we let go and allow, it may find us.

Instead of trying to "fall asleep," try:

- Allowing yourself to simply rest
- Being grateful that your body is resting, even if your mind is still awake
- Reminding yourself that both rest and sleep have value

Every moment of rest is a gift, even if it's not sleep.

CARD 2: YOU ARE SAFE IN THE DARK

Wakeful Heart,

In darkness, the mind can create frightening stories. But here, right now, in reality: You are safe. You are sheltered. You are supported by your bed. You are surrounded by four walls.

Feel the presence of the things protecting you. Your body can rest, even if your mind is busy. You are safe to relax.

Tired Heart,

Worrying about sleep can actually make sleep harder to come. Remember:

- One night of poor sleep is not a disaster
- Your body still benefits from quiet rest
- Most "catastrophic" thoughts about missing sleep are inaccurate
- We often sleep more than we think we do

Instead of trying to "force" sleep to come, allow yourself to simply rest. Be gentle with yourself, as you would with a tired child.

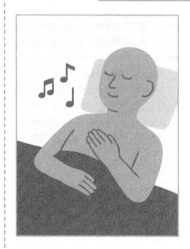

Resting Heart,

Try this relaxation exercise:

- Starting with your toes, gradually move up to the top of your head
- With each part of your body, tighten the muscles for 3 seconds, then release
- Notice the warm, heavy sensation as muscles relax
- As you relax each part, whisper "Rest" to that part

Your body has served you all day. Now is the time to let it rest. Even if the mind is still awake, the body can still rest.

CARD 5: THE LULLABY OF ANCESTORS

Night Heart,

Humans have lived through countless dark nights since the dawn of humanity. In the darkest times, our ancestors found comfort and healing.

Imagine all the people who have been awake in the night across history. You're part of this eternal stream. You are not alone in your wakefulness.

Darkness holds beauty, mystery, and rest too. This darkness is also a precious part of life.

CARD 6: CHANGING THE NIGHT STORY

Awake Heart,

When anxiety arrives in the night, it often brings exaggerated and catastrophic stories. Stories like: "I'll never get to sleep" "Tomorrow will be a disaster if I don't sleep" "Something is seriously wrong with me"

You can recognize these for what they are - just thoughts, not facts. Instead, try these stories: "My body knows how to sleep; it will sleep when it's ready" "I can cope with fatigue; I've done it before" "Simply resting has value too"

CARD 7: NIGHTTIME PRAYER

Quiet Heart,

There is something sacred about the night - a moment between today and tomorrow. A space where we can let go of all that has happened and postpone all that is to come.

In this sacred moment, imagine that you're releasing every worry, every responsibility, and every burden. Imagine you're giving them to the vast night sky to hold until morning.

In this night, your only job is to rest. Trust that the universe will continue turning while you rest.

"BREATH LULLABY" CARDS

Breath is the companion that stays with us always, from our first breath to our last. In moments of anxiety, connecting with the breath can be a simple yet powerful way to return to the present. Below are gentle reminders and guidance for the breath.

CARD 1: BREATH IS HOME

Breathing Heart,

Breath is the home you can always return to. It requires no special equipment or complex skills. It's always here, ready to welcome you.

Simply breathe in, noting: "I am breathing in." Simply breathe out, noting: "I am breathing out."

This is the simplest practice and also the most profound. Simply returning to the breath, again and again, with endless kindness.

CARD 2: 4-7-8 BREATH

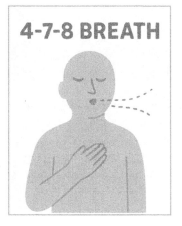

4-7-8 BREATH

Balancing Heart,

Try the 4-7-8 technique:

- Breathe in through your nose for 4 seconds
- Hold your breath for 7 seconds
- Breathe out through your mouth for 8 seconds, making a gentle "whoosh" sound

The extended exhale helps activate the parasympathetic nervous system - your body's "rest and digest" system.

Do 4 cycles like this. If you feel lightheaded, return to natural breathing. Build the practice gradually.

CARD 3: BREATH LIKE OCEAN WAVES

Resting Heart,

Imagine your breath like waves at the shoreline. As you breathe in, the wave rises onto the shore. As you breathe out, the wave recedes back to the sea.

Up... and down. In... and out. Rising... and falling.

No hurry, no forcing. Just the natural rhythm of life. Let your body breathe at its own pace.

CARD 4: COUNTING BREATH

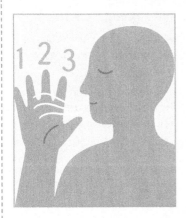

Calming Heart,

When the mind is turbulent, counting breaths can provide simple focus. Try:

Breathe in... Breathe out... Count "One"
Breathe in... Breathe out... Count "Two"
Breathe in... Breathe out... Count "Three"
Breathe in... Breathe out... Count "Four"
Breathe in... Breathe out... Count "Five"

Continue counting to 10, then start over from 1. If the mind wanders (which is completely natural), simply gently return to number 1.

CARD 5: BREATH IS LIFE

Existing Heart,

Each breath is a reminder that you are alive. Each inhale is a gift. Each exhale is a letting go.

From the moment we are born until we depart, breath accompanies us. In breath, there is connection to all living beings. In breath, there is connection to everyone who has ever lived.

Even in the most difficult moments, breath is evidence that life continues within you.

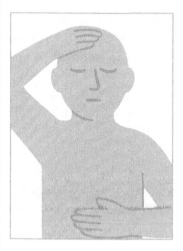

Expanding Heart,

Imagine that your breath can travel to any part of your body. Try following these steps:

- Breathe in, imagine the breath going to your shoulders
- Breathe out, imagine your shoulders releasing, relaxing
- Breathe in, send breath to your chest area
- Breathe out, feel the chest open, release
- Breathe in, send breath to your belly
- Breathe out, feel the belly soften, release

Move your attention through different parts of the body, using breath as a healing source.

Focusing Heart,

Give your breath names that can bring you to a peaceful state:

As you breathe in, silently say: "Peace" As you breathe out, silently say: "Release"

Or try: Breathing in: "I am here" Breathing out: "I am fine"

Or simply: Breathing in: "In" Breathing out: "Out"

These simple words can anchor the mind, bringing stillness amid rushed thoughts.

265

"I AM HERE WITH YOU" CARDS

Sometimes, what we need most in moments of anxiety is a sense of companionship - a gentle voice reminding us that we're not alone and that we will get through this. These cards bring the comfort of compassion for when you need it most.

CARD 1: YOU ARE NOT BROKEN

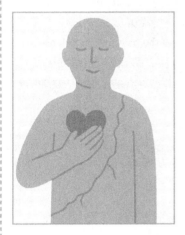

Whole Heart,

Anxiety is not a sign of weakness or defect. It is not a sign that something is "wrong" with you.

On the contrary, it shows that:

- Your natural protection systems are working
- You have the capacity to feel deeply
- You are a real human, experiencing the full spectrum of emotions

We live in a world that often demands we be "okay" all the time. But no one is "okay" all the time. Difficult emotions don't make you less; they make you human.

CARD 2: YOU ARE DOING WELL

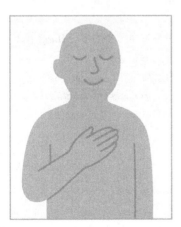

Brave Heart,

It's genuinely difficult to face anxiety. The fact that you're still trying, still breathing, still looking for ways to care for yourself - that shows extraordinary strength.

You're doing better than you think. You're handling things better than you believe. You have more capability than you imagine.

Remember: Success with anxiety isn't feeling "good" - it's continuing to move forward, even when feeling afraid. And you're doing that right now.

CARD 3: YOU DESERVE KINDNESS

Precious Heart,

Anxiety can make us harsh with ourselves – self-critical, self-blaming, and self-shaming. But it's in these moments that you need kindness the most.

Place a hand on your heart and remind yourself: "I deserve kindness, especially when I'm struggling." "I would be better served by being gentle with myself." "I'm doing the best I can with the tools I have."

Kindness isn't a reward for perfection. It's something you deserve because you're trying.

CARD 4: YOU ARE NOT YOUR ANXIETY

Dear Heart,

Anxiety is visiting you, but it is not you. You are not your thoughts. You are not your feelings. You are the one who is aware of these thoughts and feelings.

You are larger than this anxiety. You are deeper than this feeling. You are wider than this moment.

I see you behind the anxiety – the witnessing one, the holding one, the trying one. And I am here with that one.

CARD 5: PLACE US BESIDE YOU

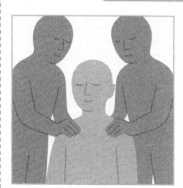

Accompanied Heart,

Imagine, just for this moment, that all who love you are sitting beside you. The people who have supported you, who have seen your strength, who have held you when you cried.

Feel their presence around you, like a protective circle. Hear their voices, reminding you of all the reasons why you deserve care.

You are never truly alone. These connections live within you, even when physical distance or time may separate.

CARD 6: WE ARE ALL CONNECTED

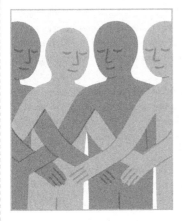

Heart Never Alone,

Right now, across the world, there are millions of people experiencing anxiety. Behind closed doors, in beds, in cars, at workplaces - countless people are feeling what you're feeling.

Although anxiety can make you feel isolated and "different", the reality is that it connects you with much of humanity. Anxiety is part of our shared human experience.

Send kindness to all those who are struggling just like you. In this invisible connection, there is strength and comfort.

CARD 7: I AM HERE WITH YOU

Accompanied Heart,

Imagine, just for this moment, that all who love you are sitting beside you. The people who have supported you, who have seen your strength, who have held you when you cried.

Feel their presence around you, like a protective circle. Hear their voices, reminding you of all the reasons why you deserve care.

You are never truly alone. These connections live within you, even when physical distance or time may separate.

HEALING PASSAGES

HEART-CENTERED MEDITATION

In moments of anxiety, our hearts need to be soothed and sheltered. Heart-centered meditation can be a powerful way to nurture a sense of safety, peace, and self-care. Below are some meditations to help you connect with and soothe your heart.

1. "NURTURING HAND" MEDITATION

Find a comfortable position, sitting or lying down. If you feel comfortable, gently close your eyes.

- Begin by placing one or both hands on the center of your chest - where your heart lies. Feel the gentle weight and warmth of your hand.

- Breathe in deeply, and as you exhale, imagine your breath moving in and out through your heart center, beneath your hand.

- As you continue to breathe, notice your heartbeat - steady, consistent, always present. This heart has been beating since before you were born and will continue to beat, moment to moment.

- Now imagine that your hand is cradling your heart as if it were a small, precious living creature. Your hand brings safety, warmth, and care.

- With each inhale, imagine you're sending love, kindness, and care into your heart. With each exhale, imagine your heart relaxing, opening, feeling supported and safe.

- Try saying these words to your heart, or create your own: "I am here with you." "I am holding you safely." "I care about this pain." "We will get through this together."

- Allow yourself to feel whatever emotions might arise. If tears come, let them flow. If anger surfaces, acknowledge it. All are welcome under the gentle touch.

- Continue breathing in and out through the heart center, letting your hand nurture your heart for another 2-3 minutes, or as long as you wish.

- When you're ready to end, gently thank yourself for taking time to care for your heart. Slowly lift your hand from your chest, but retain the feeling of nurturing and loving presence.

2. "WISE HEART" MEDITATION

Find a comfortable sitting or lying position. Allow your body to relax, and if you feel comfortable, close your eyes.

- Begin by bringing your attention to your natural breath. No need to change it - just observe the gentle rise and fall of chest and belly as air moves in and out.

- After a few breaths, shift your attention to your heart area - the space in the middle of your chest. If helpful, you can place your hand over your heart as a gesture of connection.

- Now, imagine that inside your heart is a source of deep wisdom - a part of you that knows exactly what you need, what nourishes you, and how to navigate challenges. This part of you carries understanding far beyond the anxious mind.

- As you breathe in and out through the heart area, imagine you're connecting with this innate wisdom. Feel it as a warm glow, a sense of knowing, or simply as a quiet presence.

- With an open and curious mind, try asking your wise heart a simple question: "What do I need to know right now?"

- Then, simply listen. No need to struggle or try too hard. Just create space for wisdom to emerge in its own way - it might be a word, an image, a body sensation, or a subtle intuition.

- If nothing emerges immediately, that's perfectly fine. Just continue being present, breathing, and trusting that this communication is happening at a deeper level.

- You might try another question like: "How can I best care for myself today?" or "What is the gentlest next step?"

- Allow yourself to listen for answers from this inner wisdom. Heart-answers are often gentle, kind, and simple - different from the worried, critical voice of the mind.

- Spend a few more minutes listening and connecting. When you're ready, gently place your hand on your heart in a gesture of gratitude, and slowly open your eyes.

- Record any wisdom you received, or simply remember that you can always return to this inner wisdom place.

3. "OPEN HEART" MEDITATION

Find a quiet space and a comfortable position. You may sit with a straight back or lie down, whichever feels most comfortable.

- Begin with a few deep and even breaths, allowing your body to relax with each exhale. Feel tension melting away as you breathe out.

- Now, bring your attention to your chest area. Place your hand gently on the center of your chest. Feel the warmth and the sensation of contact beneath your palm.

- Imagine that at the center of your chest there is a lotus flower of light, representing your heart. As you focus on it, the flower begins to slowly open, petals unfolding, glowing with warm light.

- With each breath, the heart flower expands more. With each exhale, feel any limitations, hardship, and defenses melting, allowing the heart to open further.

- Now, imagine the light from your heart beginning to spread - first, filling your entire chest... then spreading to your shoulders and arms... down to your stomach and lower abdomen... up to your neck and face... down to your thighs, calves, and feet.

- Allow your entire body to be bathed in the warm light from your expanding heart.

- Now, imagine the light beginning to expand beyond your body - spreading into the space around you... filling the room... extending further into the world.

- Imagine the light from your heart touching those you love... those you know... even those you find difficult... and finally, all beings across the world.

- Feel your heart connected to all hearts - in an invisible network of compassion, understanding, and kindness.

- Stay in this space for a while, allowing your heart to expand further with each breath. If the heart seems to close or contract, that's natural - simply gently invite it to open again, without judgment.

- When you're ready to end, gently bring your attention back to your body. Feel the contact with the ground or chair beneath you. Notice your breath moving in and out.

- Gently wiggle your fingers and toes, and when you feel ready, slowly open your eyes.

- Carry this sense of expansion and connection into the rest of your day - remembering that you can return to this state whenever you need.

LULLABY FOR THE TIRED BODY

When anxiety persists, our bodies too are deeply affected. Tension accumulates in muscles, stress stiffens joints, and our entire system can feel exhausted. These whole-body relaxation exercises are designed to release physical tension and bring a sense of rest and peace to the tired body.

1. BLUE LIGHT BODY SCAN

Find a comfortable place to lie down where you won't be disturbed. You may cover yourself with a light blanket if that helps you feel comfortable and protected.

- Close your eyes and begin to notice your breath. No need to change it - just let it be natural and gentle. Just notice the sensation of air moving in and out of your body.

- When you feel ready, begin to bring your attention to the top of your head. Imagine a gentle, healing blue light beginning to form there - like the most beautiful, gentle blue light you've ever seen. It could be the pale blue of the sky or the deeper blue of the ocean - whatever blue brings you a sense of peace.

- With each exhale, imagine this blue light moving down, beginning to infuse your forehead. Feel the skin and muscles in the forehead relaxing and softening as they come into contact with this light.

- Continue breathing, the blue light flowing down your face - the eye area, cheeks, jaw. Feel all the facial muscles gradually relaxing and releasing any holding or tension. Pay special attention to your jaw, allowing it to soften, perhaps slightly open.

- With the next breath, the blue light moves down to your neck and shoulders. Feel the light infusing any areas of tension, melting rigidity and strain. Feel your shoulders dropping down, away from your ears, as they relax and release.

- Now, the blue light flows down your arms, from shoulders to elbows, to wrists, and out to your fingers. Feel any tension or discomfort melting away.

- Return to the shoulders and feel the blue light moving down your chest and back. Imagine it infusing your heart, bringing a sense of safety and peace. Feel the chest opening as emotional armor softens and melts. Feel the muscles in your back relaxing and lengthening, fully supporting you.

- The light continues to move down to your abdomen. Feel the abdominal muscles softening and relaxing. Many of us hold a lot of tension in the belly area, so take a minute to let the healing blue light soak deeply into this area.

- Now the light flows down to your hips and pelvic area, bringing a sense of deep relaxation and support. Feel any tension in the hip and pelvic floor area melting away.

- The blue light continues to pour down your thighs, to your knees, down your calves, to your ankles, and finally out to your toes. Feel your legs becoming heavy and fully supported as they relax into the support beneath you.

- Now, imagine your entire body is soaking in this healing blue light. From the top of your head to your toes, every cell in your body is relaxed, soothed, and nourished.

- Feel the sensation of heaviness, warmth, and being fully supported. Feel all tension and anxiety gradually melting away, allowing your body to rest deeply.

- Rest here for a few minutes, bathing in this blue light, allowing it to seep into any areas in your body that might still need relaxation.

- When you're ready to end, begin to bring a little movement back to your fingers and toes. Take a deep, refreshing breath, feeling your body filled with new energy. Slowly open your eyes, knowing that this deep relaxation is always available to you whenever you need it.

2. PROGRESSIVE MUSCLE RELAXATION

This exercise uses a powerful relaxation technique called Progressive Muscle Relaxation, where you deliberately tense muscles and then release to create a deeper sense of relaxation.

Find a comfortable position to sit or lie down, where you can relax undisturbed for the next few minutes.

- Begin by taking three deep breaths. Inhale deeply through your nose, counting to 4, and exhale through your mouth, counting to 6. Allow each exhale to begin softening your body.

- Now, we'll work from feet to head, tensing and relaxing each muscle group in turn.

- Start with your feet. Curl your toes down and tighten the muscles in your feet tightly. Hold for 5 seconds, noticing the sensation of tension. And now - release. Allow your feet to completely relax and notice the contrasting sensation of relaxation. Feel the feet muscles becoming heavy and warm.

- Move up to your calves. Tighten your calves by pointing your toes toward you. Hold the tension for 5 seconds. And release, allowing the calves to soften completely.

- Now to your thighs. Press your thighs together or tense the thigh muscles by straightening your legs. Hold for 5 seconds. And release, feeling the thigh muscles soften and become heavy.

- Move up to your abdominal muscles. Tighten your stomach muscles, as if preparing for a punch. Hold for 5 seconds. And release, allowing the belly to soften completely with each breath.

- Now to your back. Gently arch your back, creating space between the vertebrae. Hold for 5 seconds. And release, allowing your back to be fully supported by the surface you're lying on.

- Move up to your shoulders. Lift your shoulders up toward your ears, creating major tension. Hold for 5 seconds. And release, allowing shoulders to drop down, away from the ears.

- Now to your arms. Begin by clenching your hands into tight fists. Hold for 5 seconds. Release, straightening the fingers and feeling the tension flow out.

- Next, the upper arms. Bend your elbows and tense your biceps. Hold for 5 seconds. And release, allowing the arms to become completely soft.

- Move up to your face. Begin by scrunching up all facial muscles together. Hold for 5 seconds. And release, letting the face become soft and comfortable.

- Finally, tighten your jaw by clenching your teeth together. Hold for 5 seconds. And release, letting the jaw hang slightly open, teeth not touching.

- Now, notice your entire body. Feel the deep relaxation spreading from head to toe. Enjoy the sensation of heaviness, warmth, and release.

- Take a minute to scan your entire body, looking for any areas that might still be holding tension. If you find an area, gently repeat the tense-release process for that area.

- Take a deep breath into your belly, and as you exhale, imagine you're releasing any remaining tension.

- Rest in this state of deep relaxation for a minute or longer, enjoying the feeling of peace and comfort.

- When you're ready to return, gently move your fingers and toes, take a deep refreshing breath, and slowly open your eyes, carrying this relaxation with you.

3. "SAFE REST" EXERCISE

This practice is especially helpful when the body is in a fight-or-flight state and needs to be brought back to rest and digest mode.

Find a truly comfortable position - perhaps lying on a bed, on the floor with pillows under head and knees, or in a soft chair. It's important that your body feels fully supported.

- Close your eyes or lower your gaze gently. Begin by noticing the points of contact between your body and the supporting surface below. Feel the floor, bed, or chair holding your weight. Allow these contact points to become more prominent in your awareness.

- Imagine that with each exhale, your body can release deeper into this support, as if you're melting into it. Nothing to do, nowhere to go, just allowing the surface to carry your entire weight.

- *Now, bring awareness to the feeling of safety in the present moment. Notice that in this moment:*

  + **You are sheltered by a roof**
  + **You are protected by surrounding walls**
  + **You have sufficient oxygen to breathe**
  + **Your body is supported**
  + **There are no immediate threats**

- Take a deep breath into your belly, feeling it expand as you inhale. As you exhale, send a message to your nervous system: "It's safe to rest now."

- Notice any places in the body that are still holding tension or vigilance. Often these areas include the jaw, shoulders, neck, belly, or hips. When you discover a tense area, gently whisper to it: "You can rest now. We are safe."

- Imagine that your entire body is being immersed in gentle, soothing warm water. Feel the warmth seeping into every muscle, every organ, every cell. Each exhale is an invitation for your body to release deeper into this state of rest and restoration.

- Recognize that your nervous system has served you well by trying to keep you safe. Now, you can invite it to rest, reset, and restore. Like a faithful guardian who has worked overtime, you can gently say: "Thank you for protecting me. Now you can rest."

- Maintain attention on the sensations of safety, warmth, and support. Allow natural breathing to guide you deeper into this resting state.

- Remain in this state for at least 5-10 minutes, or longer if you have time. This is a healing gift for your entire system.

- When you're ready to end, begin by bringing awareness back to the room, feeling the space around you. Then gently move your fingers and toes, perhaps stretching pleasantly.

- Note that you can access this "Safe Rest" state whenever you feel triggered, anxious, or exhausted. Even just two minutes in this state can help reset your nervous system.

JOURNEY TO A SAFE PLACE

Each of us needs a safe place - a space where we feel protected, secure, and completely at ease. While we may not always be able to find that safe place in the external world, we can always create and access an inner safe place through the power of imagination.

Below are some visualization practices to create and access a safe space within you - a sanctuary to turn to when anxiety rises.

1. CREATING A SAFE HAVEN

Find a quiet space where you won't be disturbed. Sit or lie in a comfortable position and close your eyes or lower your gaze.

- Begin by taking a little time to connect with your breath and body, just noticing the sensation of air moving in and out of your body. Allow your breathing to become slow and even.

- Now, imagine that you are in a place where you feel completely safe, peaceful, and comfortable. This could be a real place you've been to, a place from childhood memory, a place you've read about or dreamed of, or a place you completely create in your imagination.

- Take time to really build this place in your mind, making it as vivid and detailed as possible.

- *Ask yourself:*

+ *Where am I? Is it a quiet beach, a cabin in the woods, a secret garden, a cozy room, or somewhere entirely different?*

+ *What does this place look like? Notice colors, shapes, light, and shadow.*

+ *What can I hear? Perhaps it's waves lapping, leaves rustling, a crackling fire, gentle music, or maybe it's complete silence.*

+ *How does this place smell? Salty sea air, pine forest, fragrant flowers, herbal tea, or freshly baked bread?*

+ *What can I feel on my skin? The warmth of sunshine, a cool breeze, the softness of a blanket, or the coolness of grass beneath your feet?*

- Going into specific detail makes the experience more real and impactful. This is your space, so create it exactly as you want.

- After you've created this space, imagine that you are completely safe here. Nothing can disturb or harm you in this sanctuary. You are free to completely relax, dropping all defenses and vigilance.

- Take time to really feel the sensation of safety and peace spreading throughout your entire body. Feel muscles relaxing, breath slowing, and mind becoming quieter.

- *Now, ask yourself what else you might need to feel completely comfortable and safe in this space. It might be:*

    + **A special loving person (real or imagined, human or pet)**

    + **A special object that brings a sense of protection**

    + **A healing color or light surrounding the space**

    + **A sound or song that soothes your soul**

- Add any of these to your safe space. Remember that this is your space, and there are no limits to what you can create here.

- Take a moment to simply be in this safe space. Enjoy the feeling of peace, protection, and nourishment it brings. Remember that you can return to this place whenever you need to feel safe or find sanctuary from life's storms.

- When you're ready to leave, know that this space always exists within you, and you can return anytime. It will always be there, waiting for you.

- Slowly become alert again, feeling your body and the space around you. When you're ready, open your eyes, bringing the feeling of peace from your safe haven into this moment.

2. JOURNEY TO THE GARDEN OF PEACE

- Sit or lie in a comfortable position. Gently close your eyes and begin by taking a few deep, slow breaths.

- Breathe in through your nose, feeling your belly expand, and breathe out through your mouth, allowing your body to relax deeper.

- Imagine that with each exhale, you're relaxing deeper, feeling your body become heavier and supported by the surface beneath you.

- Now, imagine that you're standing before a beautiful gate. This is the entrance to your garden of peace - a secret place just for you, where you can feel completely safe, nourished, and at peace.

- When you're ready, imagine yourself pushing the gate open and stepping into the garden. The light here is perfect - not too bright, not too dark. It might be gentle afternoon sunlight filtering through leaves, or the misty light of early morning - whatever type of light makes you feel comfortable.

- Look around your garden. Notice the colors, shapes, and textures. Are there flowers? Trees? Water? Perhaps there's a small path to walk on, or a comfortable spot to rest? Create this garden according to your wishes.

- As you explore the garden, notice the scents in the air - perhaps fragrant flowers, moist earth, or freshly cut grass. Breathe deeply and let these scents soothe your senses.

- Listen to the sounds around you. You might hear gentle birdsong, rustling leaves, flowing water, or a breeze through the trees. Perhaps your garden is completely quiet, with only the sound of your breathing and heartbeat.

- Find a place in the garden that feels especially comfortable and safe to you. It might be a bench under a tree, a soft patch of grass by a pond, or a secluded corner filled with flowers.

- Go to that place and sit or lie down, feeling your body fully supported. Feel the contact of your body with the ground or surface beneath you.

- As you rest here, imagine every worry, tension, and fear melting from your body, soaking into the earth and being transformed. Feel your body and mind becoming lighter, more at ease.

- Imagine that all the air in this garden is filled with healing energy. With each inhale, you're breathing in energy of peace, kindness, and deep calm. This energy floods every cell in your body, healing and soothing from within.

- Feel the connection between your body and the garden, recognizing that the same life force that nourishes the plants also nourishes you. You are part of a larger web of life, supported and held.

- Spend time here, relaxing deeper with each breath. Nothing to do, nowhere to go, no one to be. Just being fully present in this moment, in this safe space.

- Know that you can return to this garden anytime you need. It always exists within you, a sanctuary ready to welcome you back.

- When you're ready to leave, slowly stand up and walk back to the gate. Look back at the garden one last time, carrying the peaceful feeling with you.

- As you step through the gate, begin to become aware again of the space around you. Feel your body, notice your breath, and when ready, open your eyes, bringing with you the sense of peace and refreshment.

EMBRACING FEAR

Anxiety and fear can be overwhelming emotions, and our first instinct is often to run away from or fight them. However, sometimes the most powerful approach is to embrace and contain them — learning to be with discomfort without being swept away. The practices below are designed to help you develop the ability to be with, contain, and even learn from your most difficult emotions.

1. "INVITING FEAR TO TEA" MEDITATION

Find a quiet space where you won't be disturbed. Sit comfortably, preferably with a straight but relaxed back. Gently close your eyes or lower your gaze.

- Begin by simply noticing your breath — feeling the breath coming in and going out. No need to try to change it, just observe with gentle attention and curiosity.

- After a few minutes, shift your attention to any fear or anxiety that might be present. Rather than trying to push it away or analyze it, imagine that you're inviting it to sit down with you, as if inviting a guest for tea.

- *Imagine you begin a dialogue with your fear. You might consider questions like:*

  + **"What purpose are you here for?"**
  + **"What are you trying to protect me from?"**
  + **"What might help you feel heard and understood?"**

- Note that the purpose is not to convince the fear to go away, but to create space to listen to it with curiosity and kindness. Like a difficult guest, fear often needs to be heard before it can relax.

- As you sit with the fear, notice sensations in your body. You might feel tightness in the chest, tension in the shoulders, or churning in the stomach. Rather than fighting these sensations, imagine that you're creating space for them.

- Imagine that your breath can move into and around these sensations. No need to change them, just let them be there, while you maintain a kind presence and awareness.

- If you notice yourself getting caught in stories or thoughts about the fear, gently return to the sensations in the body and your breath. Simply be with the experience, without needing to fix or change anything.

- As you continue this practice, you may notice a subtle shift. It might be tension in the body easing, the mind becoming quieter, or the fear beginning to change or move. Or there might be no change immediately, and that's perfectly okay too.

- The purpose of this practice is not to eliminate fear, but to develop a new relationship with it – one based on acceptance, understanding, and kindness, rather than opposition.

- After 10-15 minutes, or whatever time feels right for you, simply thank the fear for sharing with you, and gradually open your eyes, bringing this new understanding into your day.

2. "EXPANDING TO CONTAIN" MEDITATION

Find a comfortable position, sitting or lying, and close your eyes or gently lower your gaze.

- Begin by noticing your breath, simply feeling the natural movement of air flowing in and out.

- Gradually expand your awareness to include your entire body – feeling the posture, the contact with the supporting surface, and any sensations that are present.

- Now, bring your attention to any anxiety, fear, or discomfort that might be present. Find where this sensation is strongest in your body. It might be a choking feeling in the throat, heaviness in the chest, tension in the stomach, or elsewhere.

- As you recognize this sensation, try observing it with curiosity, as if you're learning about it for the first time. Notice its qualities – is it hot or cold? Heavy or light? Still or moving? Does it have a shape or color?

- Not to change the sensation, but just to understand it more deeply.

- Now for the main part of the practice: imagine that you are expanding the space inside yourself to contain this sensation. Rather than trying to shrink the sensation, you're creating more space around it.

- Imagine that with each inhale, you're creating more space inside. Imagine that your chest, belly, and entire body are expanding – not just physically but energetically – creating a larger space to contain your experience.

- Imagine that you can expand like the sky expands to contain even dark clouds. Nothing needs to be pushed away or changed – just creating enough space for this sensation to be present without overwhelming you.

- As you continue the practice, you may feel a subtle shift in your relationship with the discomfort. Rather than being identified with it, you're learning to contain it. You are larger than your fear; you have the capacity to hold it without being overtaken by it.

- Remember that the purpose is not to eliminate or even change the sensation, but to develop the capacity to be with it in safety and compassion. With this capacity, the sensation no longer has control.

- Continue practicing for 10-15 minutes, or as long as you wish. When you're ready to end, slowly open your eyes and carry this sense of expansion with you into the rest of your day.

CREATING
A COMFORT LIBRARY

One of the most powerful tools for coping with anxiety is a personal "comfort library" — a collection of words, quotes, and reminders that have helped you or touched your heart. These words can become trusted companions in difficult moments, reminding you of truths and wisdom when the anxious mind is spinning.

1. CREATING YOUR COMFORT LIBRARY

In the following pages, create a collection of comforting words that you can return to in moments of anxiety. These might be:

- Quotes from books, poems, or songs
- Words from loved ones or friends that have helped you
- Affirmations you've created for yourself
- Truths you want to remind yourself of when anxiety is high
- Mantras or prayers that are meaningful to you
- Wisdom from therapists, teachers, or mentors

Take time to write these words in your own handwriting. There's something very powerful about recording these words with your own hand — it creates a deeper personal connection with the wisdom they contain.

Page 1: Comforting words about fear and courage

....

....

....

....

....

....

....

....

Page 3: Comforting words about staying with difficult emotions

....

....

....

....

Page 4: Comforting words about connection and not being alone

....

....

....

....

....

....

....

2. USING YOUR COMFORT LIBRARY

Once you've created your comfort library, here are some ways you might use it:

- **IN MOMENTS OF ANXIETY:** When feeling anxiety rise, open this journal and read the comforting words. Even reading one line can help anchor your mind in truth rather than fear.

- **DAILY PRACTICE:** Consider reading one comforting word each morning as part of your morning ritual, establishing a foundation of calm for the new day.

- **MEMORIZATION:** Choose one or two particularly meaningful comforts and memorize them. This way, you always carry this healing wisdom with you.

- **SHARING:** When appropriate, share these comforts with others who might benefit from them. Healing wisdom can be multiplied when shared.

- **CONTINUE ADDING:** Your comfort library is never "finished." As you encounter new words that bring peace or insight, add them to your collection.

RESOURCE MAP

Anxiety often makes us forget the resources and strengths we have available to us. A "Resource Map" is a visual tool to remind you of all the resources – both internal and external – that you can draw upon when feeling anxious, afraid, or overwhelmed.

1. CREATING YOUR RESOURCE MAP

In the space below, you'll create a visual "map" of your resources and treasures. This can be done in many ways — a literal map with paths and locations, a "mind map" with connecting branches, or a collection of visual images and words. There's no wrong way to do this!

To help you get started, consider including these types of "treasures" (and add any other types that are meaningful to you):

Inner Treasures:

• Personal strengths and qualities you can rely on
• Coping skills you've developed
• Wisdom you've gained from past challenges
• Values that guide you
• Inner sources of peace (like breath, mindfulness, faith)

External Treasures:

• People you can reach out to for support
• Physical spaces that bring a sense of safety
• Activities that help you feel peace
• Tools and resources (like this journal, books, apps)
• Professionals or services for support

Nature Treasures:

• Natural features you find peace in (water, trees, sky)
• Animals you find comfort in
• Weather or seasons that bring restoration
• Elements (earth, water, fire, air) that bring balance

Spiritual/Soul Treasures:

• Religious or spiritual practices that bring peace
• Connection to something larger than yourself
• Sacred stories or teachings that provide guidance
• Rituals or ceremonies that bring a sense of rootedness or meaning

Present your map in a way that feels visual and meaningful to you. Use colors, drawings, words, or symbols – anything that helps make it come alive and feel personal.

As you create your map, think about how each of these "treasures" has helped you in the past, and specifically how you might access it in the future. The more specific, the better.

2. USING YOUR RESOURCE MAP

• **PAY TRIBUTE TO LIFE COMPANIONS.** Place this map where you'll see it regularly. This reminds you that you have more resources than you think.

• **IN MOMENTS OF ANXIETY.** When you feel anxious or overwhelmed, look at the map and choose a specific "treasure" to access. Sometimes, just knowing you have options reduces the sense of helplessness that anxiety can bring.

• **SHARE WITH SUPPORTERS.** Consider sharing this map with a trusted friend, family member, or therapist. They can help you remember your treasures when you feel disconnected from them.

• **CONTINUE DEVELOPING.** Your resource map is a living document. As you discover new resources or realize ones you've overlooked, add them. Your treasures will grow as you continue your journey.

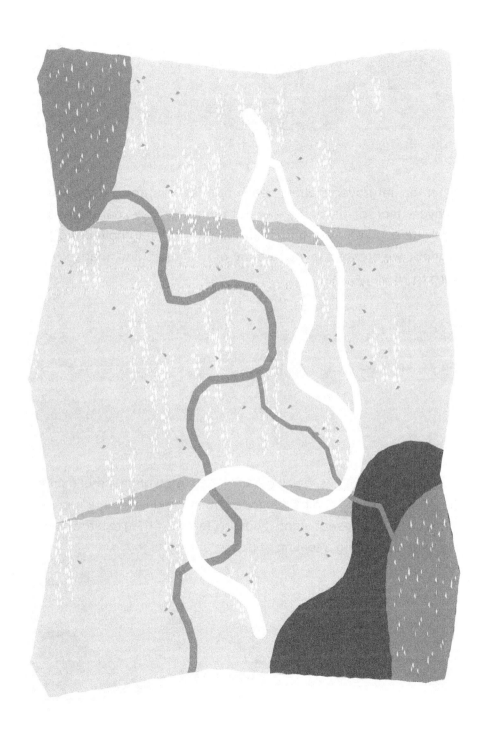

ALBUM OF PEACEFUL MOMENTS

When anxiety overwhelms, peace can feel distant or inaccessible. However, each of us has "peaceful moments" – experiences when we felt safe, comforted, and calm. By intentionally collecting these moments, we create a living "album" of memories and images we can return to when needed.

CREATING YOUR ALBUM OF PEACEFUL MOMENTS

1. CREATING YOUR COMFORT LIBRARY

In the following pages, you'll create a collection of peaceful moments from your life. These can be memories from any time in your life – from childhood to the present – and it doesn't matter if they're large or small, as long as they bring a feeling of peace, safety, or joy.

Page 1: Moments in Nature Describe a time when connecting with nature brought you a sense of peace or warmth. It might be a beautiful sunset, a walk in the forest, the feeling of ocean waves at your feet, or gazing at a starry sky.

Try to describe all the sensory details — what you saw, smelled, heard, and felt. Be as specific as possible.

....

....

....

....

Page 2: Moments of Connection Describe a meaningful moment of connection with another that brought peace or joy. It might be an intimate conversation with a friend, a hug from a loved one, a warm family meal, or even a moment of connection with a stranger that touched your heart.

....

....

....

....

....

Page 3: Moments of Achievement Describe a time when you felt a sense of accomplishment, pride in yourself, or capability. It might be completing a goal, overcoming a challenge, or simply experiencing a moment when you handled a situation really well.

....

....

....

....

Page 4: Moments of Stillness Describe a moment of complete stillness — a time when your mind and body felt peaceful and relaxed. It might be a moment of waking up early when the house is still quiet, a deep meditation experience, or quiet time alone you cherished.

....

....

....

....

Page 5: Small Perfect Moments Sometimes, the most peaceful moments are the smallest ones — everyday moments easy to overlook but containing subtle joy. Describe a small but "perfect" moment from your daily life — it might be the taste of morning coffee, sunlight streaming through a window in a particular way, or the feeling of a cool pillow against your cheek.

....

....

....

3. USING YOUR ALBUM OF PEACEFUL MOMENTS

Here are some ways to use your album of peaceful moments after you've created it:

- **SANCTUARY IN THE STORM:** When anxiety runs high, read through these moments to remind yourself that peace is possible and is part of your experience. When the present moment feels unbearable, recalling peaceful moments from the past can bring hope.

- **GUIDED VISUALIZATION:** Choose one of your peaceful moments and use it as a visualization exercise. Close your eyes and imagine yourself returning to that moment, using all your senses to make it vivid. This can trigger the same relaxation response in your body as the original experience.

- **INTENTIONAL SEEKING:** Once you've identified the types of moments that bring you peace, actively seek out more such moments in your daily life. Your album can become a "treasure map" to experiences that nourish you.

- **GRATITUDE FOCUS:** Flip through this album as a gratitude practice, giving thanks for the peaceful moments that have been part of your life and will come in the future.

- **SHARE THE PEACE:** When appropriate, share one of your peaceful moments with others. Sometimes, talking about these moments can help reinforce and deepen the sense of peace they bring.

Sometimes, our deepest experiences — including our experiences with anxiety and healing — cannot be fully accessed through logical or analytical language. Poetry, creative writing, and storytelling provide another way to understand and transform our experience.

In this space, you're invited to explore your creative voice — to write a poem, short story, letter, or any other form of expression that helps you to visualize and transform your journey with anxiety.

CREATIVE WRITING PROMPTS

Here are some prompts to help you get started. You can choose one of these or follow your own creative inspiration:

1. POETRY

- Write a short poem titled "Anxiety Is Not My Enemy"
- Create a two-voiced poem — with one voice being anxiety and the other being compassion
- Write a haiku (3-line poem with syllable pattern 5-7-5) about a moment of peace
- Write a poem about what anxiety has taught you
- Create a poem titled "My Heart Knows the Way"

2. STORYTELLING AND CREATIVE WRITING

- Write a letter from your wise and compassionate self to your self that is struggling with anxiety
- Create a short story where your anxiety is personified as a character
- Write about a moment when you felt completely at peace, going into every sensory detail
- Imagine and describe a day in the future when your relationship with anxiety has transformed
- Write a "personal myth" – a parable-like story explaining your journey with anxiety using symbolic language

3. USING CREATIVE EXPRESSION

After you've written your poems, stories, or other creative expressions, here are some ways you might use them:

- **DEEPER SELF-UNDERSTANDING:** Reread what you've written and notice what themes, symbols, or insights emerge. Sometimes, through creative expression, our inner wisdom appears in unexpected ways.

- **SHARE IF YOU FEEL COMFORTABLE:** If appropriate, share what you've written with a trusted person or therapist. This might open up conversation and new understanding.

- **CONTINUE DEVELOPING:** If a particular poem or story seems especially meaningful or healing, consider expanding it, editing it, or using it as a starting point for further creative expression.

- **TRANSFORMATION RITUAL:** If you've written about a painful aspect of anxiety, you might perform a simple ritual (like reading it aloud, then safely burning the paper – following proper safety regulations) as a symbolic act of release or transformation.

- **READ WHEN NEEDED:** Keep creative writings that help you feel comforted, empowered, or insightful, and return to them when you need to be reminded of your inner wisdom.

Creative Space Page: Use the space below to write your poem, story, or other creative expression. There are no rules here — this is your space to explore, experiment, and express.

....

....

....

Ending Part III

As we conclude this "Toolkit from the Heart" section, remember that no tool works for everyone in every moment. Allow yourself to explore, experiment, and discover what works best for you. Some tools may feel immediately helpful, while others may become more meaningful as you practice them over time.

This toolkit is not a rigid set of skills to "fix" anxiety, but a collection of whispers from the heart, invitations to connect more deeply with yourself, and spaces you can return to when needed. These are gifts from heart to heart – a reminder of the wisdom and strength that already lives within you.

As you continue your journey, remember that healing is not a straight line but a spiral. We move forward, circle back, and sometimes seem to return to where we started – only to discover that we're at the same point but at a deeper level, with more understanding and compassion.

Carry this toolkit in your heart, knowing it's always there when you need it.

FAREWELL AND RESOURCES

PART 4

FAREWELL

LOOKING BACK ON THE JOURNEY

We've come a long way together. From the first pages to this moment, you've made a profound commitment to your journey of self-care and healing.

Looking back over these 90 days, you may notice many subtle shifts and transformations. There may have been days when you eagerly turned the pages of this journal, and days when simply opening it was a challenge. Each day, each moment with this journal, was a step in your journey — not always easy, but always worthwhile.

Take some time to reflect on your journey:

- **SIGNIFICANT MOMENTS:** What discoveries, insights, or breakthrough moments emerged on this journey?

- **CHALLENGES:** What difficulties did you encounter, and how did you navigate them?

- **SHIFTS:** What changes have you noticed in how you experience and respond to anxiety?

- **VALUABLE TOOLS:** Which practices, techniques or insights have supported you the most?

- **WHO YOU'RE BECOMING:** How have you grown or changed over these 90 days?

[Space for drawing/writing]

SEEDS HAVE BEEN PLANTED

The path of self-care and healing anxiety isn't a destination but a journey that continues to unfold. The work you've done over these 90 days has planted valuable seeds for ongoing growth.

Some seeds have already sprouted, and you've witnessed changes. Others are still developing beneath the soil, not yet visible but still growing. And some may not have begun to germinate yet, waiting for the right season and timing.

Each page you completed, each moment of awareness you experienced, each conscious breath you took – all are part of the inner garden you're cultivating. Nothing in this process is wasted, even the days of struggle or times when you may have set the journal aside.

Reflect on the seeds you've planted:

- **SEEDS OF MINDFULNESS:** The ability to notice thoughts, emotions, and sensations without judgment or identification

- **SEEDS OF SELF-COMPASSION:** Kindness toward yourself, especially when in pain or struggling

- **SEEDS OF COURAGE:** Willingness to face fears and difficult situations rather than avoiding them

- **SEEDS OF SELF-KNOWLEDGE:** Deeper understanding of yourself, your triggers, and what nourishes you

- **SEEDS OF PEACE:** The ability to find moments of calm even amid the storm

As you continue into the days, weeks, and months ahead, remember that the work of tending these seeds continues. Sometimes, that means intentional practices. Other times, it means simply allowing the process to unfold, trusting the innate wisdom of your heart and body.

[Space for drawing/writing]

YOUR HEART KNOWS THE WAY

As we come to the end of this 90-day journey, I want to share one of the deepest and often overlooked truths about anxiety and the healing process: your heart knows the way.

Amid all the advice, techniques, and methods, we can sometimes lose touch with the innate wisdom within us — a part of us that knows exactly what we need, if we're willing to listen.

Anxiety often makes us doubt our capabilities, causing us to seek answers externally. But as you've learned to listen more deeply to your heart, you may discover that many of the answers you seek have been within you all along.

This doesn't mean you don't need support, guidance, or resources. All have their place. But it's a reminder that the ultimate authority in your life is you — you with all the wisdom, intuition, and understanding you're developing every day.

In moments of confusion, when you're not sure where to go next or what to do next, remember that you can turn inward, place a hand on your heart, and ask: "Dear heart, what do we need right now?" And then, allow yourself to trust the answer that emerges.

Sometimes, the answer will come as words. Other times, it will be a feeling in your body, an image, or a memory. And sometimes, the answer will simply be "I don't know right now, and that's okay."

In these final pages, I invite you to dialogue with your heart:

My heart, what is the most important thing I need to remember as I continue this journey?

....

....

....

....

....

My heart, how can I continue to nurture and support you?

....

....

....

....

....

My heart, what do you want me to know that I may not have been listening to?

....

....

....

....

....

RESOURCES WITH HEART

COMPANION BOOKS

This journal has been a companion to you over the past 90 days. As you continue your path, you might find value in seeking additional companions in the form of books.

Below are some books described not as dry clinical texts, but as friends — each with their own personality and gifts.

1. BOOKS ON UNDERSTANDING ANXIETY

"Daring Greatly" by Brené Brown **Like your brave and authentic friend**

This friend will encourage you to look straight at fear and vulnerability with courage and powerful authenticity. Brown shares personal stories alongside research on vulnerability, showing that what we often think of as weaknesses are actually our greatest sources of strength. This book is the friend who will hold your hand as you step into unexplored spaces with courage.

"The Body Keeps the Score" by Bessel van der Kolk **Like the friend who understands the connection between your mind and body**

This friend speaks with profound understanding about how our bodies carry our stories — particularly stories of trauma and anxiety. While sometimes a bit complex for some readers (like that smart friend who speaks in technical terms), this book provides deep insights into how our minds, brains, and bodies interact, and how to heal this relationship.

"Anxiety: The Missing Stage of Grief" by Claire Bidwell Smith Like the friend who understands the connection between loss and anxiety

This is the gentle friend who will take your hand to explore the profound and often overlooked connection between anxiety and all forms of loss in life — from death of loved ones to job loss, moving, or even shifts in personal identity. Smith shares personal experience alongside wisdom from her work as a grief counselor to help us understand that anxiety is often a natural response to unresolved loss.

2. BOOKS ON HEALING AND TRANSFORMATION

"When Things Fall Apart" by Pema Chödrön Like the friend who has weathered storms and found openness

This friend speaks from a place of profound understanding and clarity, sharing Buddhist wisdom in an accessible, relaxed, and immensely practical way for difficult times. Chödrön teaches us how to "lean into" fear rather than run from it, and how to find softness rather than rigidity when facing whatever life brings. This book is the kind but honest friend who will meet you exactly where you are, while inviting you to a more spacious and free place.

"Self-Compassion" by Kristin Neff Like the friend who teaches you to treat yourself with kindness

This friend will help you develop a better relationship with yourself, especially during times of struggle. Neff combines research, personal stories, and practical exercises to show you how to treat yourself with the same kindness you would offer a good friend. This book speaks to you like a friend who loves you unconditionally and wants to help you love yourself in the same way.

"Peace Is Every Step" by Thich Nhat Hanh Like the gentle friend walking beside you

This is the calm and centered friend, reminding you of the simple power of being present in each moment. Thich Nhat Hanh shares simple techniques for bringing mindfulness into every aspect of daily life — from washing dishes to dealing with strong emotions. This book is like a quiet companion, always present and deeply listening.

3. BOOKS ON BUILDING A FULLER LIFE

"Radical Acceptance" by Tara Brach Like the friend who accepts you completely

This friend sits with you in complete acceptance — no judgment, no conditions — while you explore how to accept every aspect of yourself and your experience. Brach combines Buddhist wisdom with psychological understanding to guide you beyond the "trance of unworthiness," as she calls it, into wholehearted presence. This book is the friend who will accompany you in facing the most uncomfortable parts of yourself and your experience, soothing you with compassion and delight.

"The Happiness Trap" by Russ Harris Like the practical friend who helps you out of mind traps

This friend will show you in a practical, straightforward way how our efforts to achieve "happiness" can often make us feel worse. Based on Acceptance and Commitment Therapy (ACT), Harris teaches how to "unhook" from difficult thoughts and feelings rather than fighting them. This book is full of relatable metaphors and practical exercises, like that practical friend who's always ready to suggest a new approach when you're stuck.

"Untamed" by Glennon Doyle Like the friend who encourages you to live your truth

This is the friend who will wake you up in moments when you've forgotten the power and joy in living your authentic self. With painful honesty, Doyle shares her journey from trying to meet others' expectations to honoring her inner voice and intuition. This book is the brave, straight-talking friend holding your hand as you step into the most authentic version of your life.

APPS & PODCASTS

In today's digital world, we have many resources to support our journey with anxiety. Here are some apps and podcasts described in personal, accessible language.

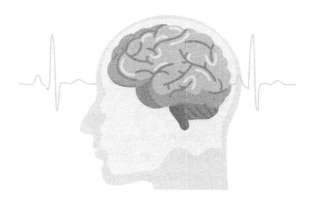

1. APPS

Calm Like the quiet friend always in your pocket

This app offers a variety of guided meditations, sleep stories, focus music, and peaceful nature sounds. The simple, accessible interface makes it a perfect companion for moments when you need to return to calm. The "Breath Bubble" feature is particularly excellent for rebalancing breath and mind when anxiety rises.

Headspace Like the cheerful, friendly meditation guide

With narrator Andy Puddicombe known for his calm, accessible voice, Headspace makes meditation simple and even fun. Structured courses by level make it easy for beginners to enter the world of meditation, yet there's enough depth for more experienced practitioners. Beautiful animations and non-mystical approach make this app approachable, like a friend who always encourages you without ever pressuring you.

Insight Timer Like a community library of peace and insight

With a massive collection of over 100,000 free meditations, mostly contributed by teachers from around the world, Insight Timer is like a global community library of peace and insight. You can find anything from simple 5-minute breathing exercises to hour-long deep meditations. Daily live sessions and community groups also bring a sense of connection, reminding you that there's a whole community of people also walking their mindfulness paths.

Simple Habit Like the friend who understands your busy schedule

Designed for busy people, Simple Habit focuses on short meditations (often 5 minutes) tailored to specific situations and needs. Whether it's stress before a presentation, trouble sleeping, or anxiety on public transport, this app has a concise, focused meditation dedicated to that situation. This is the friend who understands your busy life and helps you find moments of mindfulness in your packed schedule.

Waking Up (Sam Harris) Like the intellectual friend who will challenge and deepen your practice

Created by neuroscientist and philosopher Sam Harris, Waking Up doesn't just teach you how to meditate but why. Daily meditations combine with talks on consciousness, awareness, and other related concepts from science and philosophy. This app is well-suited for those who appreciate a meditation approach with a scientific lens and evidence-based methods. This is the friend who will challenge you to question your assumptions about mind, consciousness, and self.

Ten Percent Happier with Dan Harris Like a conversation with a straight-talking, healthily skeptical friend about mindfulness

Hosted by Dan Harris, a former ABC news reporter who discovered mindfulness after having a panic attack on live television, this podcast features straightforward and often humorous conversations with mindfulness teachers, psychologists, and others in the mental wellness field. Dan's practical, no-nonsense tone and skeptical but open approach make it ideal for those who might be suspicious of "mindfulness hype" but want to learn how to live less anxiously.

On Being with Krista Tippett Like a deep conversation with a wise friend about what it means to be human

This podcast is a series of thoughtful interviews about the meaning of being human and how we live our lives. With guests ranging from poet Mary Oliver to theoretical physicist and meditator Arthur Zajonc, Krista brings us into warm, insightful conversations not just about dealing with anxiety but about finding meaning and living fully in a world that's often challenging. This isn't a podcast specifically about anxiety, but it consistently provides insights and perspectives that soothe anxious hearts.

Unlocking Us with Brené Brown Like confiding in your most courageous and vulnerable friend

Brené Brown is known for her research on vulnerability, courage, shame, and empathy, and her podcast delves into exploring these human experiences. With her characteristic directness and authenticity, Brené and her guests (from psychologists to musicians, writers, and changemakers) discuss ways to live, love, and work more courageously. Since anxiety often stems from fear of not being loved or worthy, these frank conversations about courage and vulnerability can be healing gifts.

Anxiety Slayer Like a steadfast friend specializing in calming anxiety

Created specifically for people living with anxiety, panic attacks, and stress, this podcast provides relaxation techniques, insights about anxiety, and weekly meditations. Hosts Shann and Ananga have particularly soothing and reassuring voices, making this podcast a safe destination when you're having difficult moments. They combine insights from Western psychology with Eastern wisdom, creating a podcast that is practical and yet nurturing.

The Anxiety Coaches Podcast Like a friendly and encouraging personal coach for anxiety

Gina Ryan, who overcame chronic anxiety and panic herself, shares insights from personal experience and professional knowledge. With over 700 episodes, this podcast delves into nearly every aspect of anxiety — from social anxiety to health anxiety, from OCD to PTSD. Gina has a practical, doable, and non-judgmental approach, making the work of healing anxiety feel manageable and less lonely.

WHEN TO SEEK SUPPORT

On the journey with anxiety, there are times when we need external support. This isn't a sign of failure or weakness, but a courageous act of self-care. Just as we would seek medical support for persistent physical pain, seeking help for mental distress is equally important.

1. SIGNS IT MIGHT BE TIME TO SEEK SUPPORT

The following signs are not meant to diagnose, but simply helpful indicators of when you might benefit from some professional support:

- **ANXIETY IS AFFECTING YOUR DAILY LIFE** - Difficulty sleeping, changes in eating, trouble concentrating, or feeling overwhelmed by ordinary tasks

- **YOU'RE AVOIDING IMPORTANT OR MEANINGFUL ACTIVITIES** - Declining social opportunities, not engaging in hobbies, or avoiding situations due to anxiety

- **ANXIETY IS PERSISTENT OR LARGELY UNPREDICTABLE** - Feeling anxious most of the time, or being caught by unpredictable panic attacks

- **YOU'RE RELYING ON UNHEALTHY BEHAVIORS TO COPE** Using alcohol, drugs, overeating or undereating, or other behaviors to numb or distract yourself

- **THOUGHTS OF HARMING YOURSELF OR FEELING LIFE ISN'T WORTH LIVING** - These are clear signs to seek help immediately

- **ANXIETY FEELS TOO MUCH TO HANDLE ALONE** - Sometimes, the best measure is your internal feeling that you could use some support

Remember, the "right" time to seek help is whenever you feel you need it. You don't need to reach a "rock bottom" or crisis to deserve support.

2. TYPES OF SUPPORT AVAILABLE

Therapist/Psychologist Therapists and psychologists are trained to help you explore patterns of thoughts, emotions, and behaviors that contribute to your anxiety. They can provide a safe space to understand and address root causes, as well as teach strategies to manage and reduce anxiety. Evidence-based treatments for anxiety include Cognitive Behavioral Therapy (CBT), Acceptance and Commitment Therapy (ACT), and Exposure Therapy for certain types of anxiety.

Psychiatrist Psychiatrists are medical doctors specializing in mental health. They can assess biological aspects of anxiety and, if appropriate, prescribe medication. They often work in tandem with therapists, providing a multi-faceted approach to healing.

Support Groups Support groups, whether in-person or online, connect you with others experiencing similar challenges. This can reduce the sense of isolation that often accompanies anxiety and provide practical wisdom from people who understand it from direct experience.

Health/Mindfulness Coach Coaches can provide guidance and accountability as you develop new habits and coping methods. While they generally don't treat mental health issues, they can be a valuable part of your broader support system.

Apps and Online Resources Many apps and online programs provide evidence-based tools for managing anxiety. While not a replacement for therapy, they can be helpful and affordable adjuncts.

Crisis Helplines Crisis helplines and text services are available 24/7 for those needing immediate support. 988 (in the US) is the National Suicide Prevention Lifeline, providing free and confidential support for people in distress or emotional crisis.

3. FINDING HELP THAT WORKS FOR YOU

Seeking support should be an empowering experience, not one of barriers. Here are some considerations:

- **TRUST THE FIT:** Feeling comfortable and safe with your therapist or doctor is important. Don't hesitate to try a few providers until you find the right match.

- **TALK ABOUT COST:** Many therapists offer sliding scale payments. Some insurance programs include mental health services, and there may be community organizations offering services at reduced costs.

- **CONSIDER MULTIPLE OPTIONS:** Online therapy has expanded access to mental health care, offering more options than ever in providers, schedules, and pricing.

- **START WHERE YOU FEEL COMFORTABLE:** If one-on-one therapy feels too big a first step, start with a support group, app, workbook, or online resource.

Finally, remember that seeking help isn't a sign that you've failed in your healing journey. Instead, it's a sign that you're listening to your needs and actively seeking resources to support your growth and well-being. That's a profound act of self-respect.

WORDS FROM THE AUTHOR

PERSONAL JOURNEY

Before closing this journal, I want to share something with you: I know anxiety not just from research and professional training, but from deep personal experience.

Anxiety has been an uninvited companion in my life since I was young. As I grew up, it wore many different costumes – perfectionism worry, health anxiety, panic attacks that would wake me in the middle of the night, and the particular fear that I wasn't enough.

Around my early 30s, my anxiety reached a peak. Though from the outside, my life looked "perfect," inside, I was often coping with feelings of dread. Panic attacks became more frequent. I developed elaborate safety rituals. And I became very, very good at hiding all of this.

My turning point wasn't a single moment, but a series of small steps. Finally seeking therapy. Learning not to try to "fix" every difficult emotion immediately. Approaching mindfulness and self-compassion practices. And most importantly, beginning to talk openly about my experience – first with close friends and family, and then, as I felt safer, with more people.

What I, and so many others I've worked with, discovered was this: anxiety truly is part of the human experience. It's not an enemy to conquer. Nor is it a weakness or defect of self. In fact, sensitive, intuitive, creative, imaginative, intelligent, thoughtful, emotionally intelligent and deep people often experience anxiety. It's the other side of those wonderful qualities!

Today, I still experience anxiety. But I'm no longer afraid of it like I once was. I don't identify with it or let it define me. I've learned to make space for it, listen for the wisdom that might truly lie beneath, and honor it without letting it drive my decisions.

I share this with you because I want you to know that the person who wrote these words understands anxiety – not in an abstract way, but specifically, personally, and deeply. I've walked this journey, and I continue to walk it every day.

WHY I CREATED THIS JOURNAL

I created this journal because I believe that people living with anxiety deserve a gentle companion – something clearly different from standard quick-fix problem solving guides or dry clinical manuals. I wanted to create something that felt like a kind and understanding friend along the journey, acknowledging that healing anxiety isn't about getting rid of it entirely, but developing a new, wiser, and gentler relationship with it.

I've put into this journal all the tools, practices, and wisdom that have helped me and countless others transform their relationship with anxiety. They come from many different traditions – from modern psychology to ancient spiritual wisdom – because I believe there's no one approach that works for everyone. Anxiety can present differently in each person, and so can the path to healing.

My goal was not to "cure" you, but to create a safe space within which you could meet yourself – including your fears and anxieties – with more awareness, compassion, and wisdom. I hope these pages have supported you in that.

EMBRACING YOU FROM AFAR

As we come to the final words in this journal, I want to take a moment to acknowledge your journey. Whether you followed every exercise in this journal or only read a few pages, each step you've taken toward awareness and healing is a medal of courage.

Remember that this journey has no final destination. Even the most revered meditators, wisest psychologists, and most peaceful souls continue to grow, learn, and sometimes struggle. Being human means continually becoming.

If you're reading these lines and feel that you've changed – even just a little – in how you relate to your anxiety, that's truly a wonderful gift. If you've learned how to make a bit more space for difficult emotions, found practices that bring you back to the present, or developed a voice of self-compassion, then seeds of healing have sprouted.

Carry the wisdom and self-compassion you've cultivated here into each day as you continue. Know that you're never truly alone in this journey; you're connected to countless others also learning to live more wisely and kindly with their anxiety. My heart is embracing yours from afar, and I know that all the other hearts in this larger anxiety community are doing the same.

Go gently with yourself, and remember that you both have answers within you and have the right to seek support. Both are signs of true strength.

With love and deep understanding,

Sophia Grace

Dear Friend,

Thank you for allowing me to accompany you on this 90-day journey. Each page you've turned, each moment you've dedicated to yourself represents brave steps on your path to reclaiming inner peace.

Anxiety often makes us feel alone, but the truth is that many people are walking a similar journey to yours. Sharing your experience—whether it's joy, challenges, or small discoveries—can make an enormous difference for others seeking peace.

A Helping Hand

If this journal has accompanied you in any way, I would be deeply grateful if you could take a few minutes to share your experience. Each sincere review will help others who are seeking support find this resource.

Leaving a review is simple:

1. Visit the product page where you purchased the book (Amazon, etc.) (Or scan the QR code below to go directly to the review page.)

2. Share your honest experience with Anxiety Reset.

3. Submit your review with just a few heartfelt words.

An Embrace From Afar

Every small step you take matters. I believe that as you continue to practice self-compassion and nurture your inner space, you will find the strength and peace you deserve.

Whenever anxiety appears, remember that you are not alone and you have the tools to accompany it.

With deep gratitude and compassion,

Sophia Grace

"When you share your light, you not only illuminate

the path for others, but you also allow their light to shine."

Made in United States
North Haven, CT
23 July 2025

70964360R00183